with other possessions to ye value of 500. marks to the Abbeie of Glastenbury.

More then 600. yeares after his death, to wit about the yeere of Christ, 1189. which was the last yeere of the raigne of King Henry ye second, See ? his body was found, buryed in the Churchyard betwixt 2 pillars, xvi. foote deepe vnder ground, but those that digged the ground there to finde his bodie, after they hadde entred about 7. foote deepe into the earth, they found a mighty broad stone, with a leaden Crosse fastened to that part which lay downe wardes towardes the corpes, contayning this inscription.

Hic iacet sepultus inclitus rex Arturius in insula Aualonia.

This inscription was grauen on that side of the Crosse which was next to the stone, so that till the Crosse was taken from the stone, it was not seene. His body was foūd, not inclosed within a tombe of stōe, but within a great tree made hollowe like a trough, the which beeing digged vp and opened, therein was found the bones of Arthur, which were of a maruelous bignes, as Giraldus Cambrensis, a learned man that then lined, reporteth to haue heard of the Abbot of Glastenbury, of whome he was enformed that the shin-bone of Arthur being set vp by the leg of a very tal man came aboue his knee ye breadth of three fingers. The skull of his head of a wonderfull bignesse, in the which head there appeared the prints of x. woundes or mortall the which were growne into one seame, except onely that whereof he dyed, which beeing greater then the other appeared very plaine. Also in opening the tombe of his wife Guineuer, that was buryed with him, they found ye tresses of her haire whole and perfect, finely platted, of colour like to gold, but being touched fell to dust: the Abbot of that house (sometime Prior of Bermonsey) was named Henry Bloys, and was nephew to King Henry the second, by whose commandement the buryall of Arthur was searched for and found. Whose bones, with the bones of Guineuer his wife being found, were remooued into the new great Church (for the old was burned in Anno. 1171.) and there buried in a fayre Tombe of Marble, laying the bones of the king at the head of the Tombe, and the bones of the Queene at his foote toward the West. The Crosse of leade with the inscription, as it was found, and taken off the stone, was kept in ye treasury or reuestrey of Glastenbury Church, til the suppression thereof, in the rayghne of King Henry the eyght.

The discovery of Arthur's grave.

THE LIFE OF ARTHUR

General of the Britons

Tim Haldon

Lundarien Press

Published by Lundarien Press, UK
Copyright © Tim Haldon 2015

ISBN 978-1-910816-18-9

The right of Tim Haldon to be identified as the author of this work has been asserted in accordance with the Copyright, Designs and Patents Act 1988

<u>Cover Photograph</u>
King's Oven Cairn. The "Oven" was formerly "Arthur's Oven" and, though the remains are scant, thought to be a smelting house. French monks were told in 1113 that this vicinity was Arthur's own land.

To the memory
of
Nicholas Robinson

A good man and good friend

I see the seahorse come to his rendezvous . . .
Making the seashore shake with terror.
He is white as shining snow; he bears on his forehead horns of silver.
The water bubbles under him, in the fire of the thunder from his nostrils.
Two seahorses accompany him, as close as the grass on the edge of the pond ....

(Prophecy of Cian)

The third deep matter for the wise one:
    the blessing of Arthur
    - Blessed Arthur –
    with harmonious song,
    - a defence in battle,
    Stamping on nine.
Who are the three foremost youths who guarded the land?
Who are the three story-tellers
Who preserved the portents?

(Teyrnon's Chair)

For the memory of so
hopeless a collapse of the
island and *its unlooked for*
rescue stuck in the
minds of those who witnessed
both extraordinary events.

(Gildas, on the Downfall of Britain)

CONTENTS

Preface	ix
Chapter 1 - How books get written	1
Chapter 2 - Arthur's beginnings	4
Chapter 3 - Arthur, Cei, and Bedwyr	7
Chapter 4 - Britain 383 – 412	11
Chapter 5 - Britain 425 – 429	16
Chapter 6 - Britain 430 – 446	19
Chapter 7 - The Continental Picture	26
Chapter 8 - The Continent 451	29
Chapter 9 - The Continent 452 – 465	36
Interlude: Cian, the lost Breton bard	43
Chapter 10 - Britain 452 - 467	49
Chapter 11 - Arthur in Britain - The battle-list	55
Chapter 12 - Déols and Riothamus	61
Chapter 13 - Mount Badon	67
Chapter 14 - The Arthurian Peace	86
Chapter 15 - Continental Affairs 470 - 496	95
Chapter 16 - Arthur's Friends and Relatives	99
Chapter 17 - Camlan: why and where	108
Chapter 18 - The battle of Camlan and Arthur's Grave	117
Chapter 19 - The historical and literary aftermaths	128
Envoi	143

Appendices:

1) A Note on the Author's Speculative Method	147
2) Dating Arthur's Birth	150
3) The Last Legions in Britain	151
4) Hengest and Hnaef	154
5) The letter to Aetius	155
6) Arthur in Carlisle	157

7) The Date of the Battle of Mount Badon	159
8) (South) Cadbury Castle	162
9) A Westcountry visitor from Constantinople	165
10) Lancelot	167
11) Arthurian Sites in Devon	170
12) "Quoit" Contests	173
13) Two further combats: Mont St Michel and Mount Ar(a)wy	175
14) Arthurian Artefacts	179
15) Parley to Violence: The Raid of the Reidswire	181
16) La Villemarqué's Rehabilitation	183
17) On the Genuineness of Cian's Prophecy	186
18) La Villemarqué's other ballads	189
19) The Battle of Saint-Cast	192
Postscript	194
The Royal Dynasty of Kent	208
Families of Vortigern and Ambrosius	211
Royal Dumnonian Genealogy	213
The Descents from Cunedda	214
Maps	215
A summary life of Arthur	218
Sources for Arthur and his circle	220
Glossary	227
Some Variant names	232
Chronology	233
Further reading	237
General acknowledgements	239
Acknowledgements to translators	240
Supplementary Notes	241
Index	257

Numerals 1-27 indicate Supplementary Notes (pages 241ff)

PREFACE

The Arthur of whom I wish to speak was a 5th century British leader in post-Roman Britain and Roman northern France, of an aristocratic family, and speaking the British language, Brythonic, one related to but distinct from Irish Gaelic, as well as speaking the language of the Romans, Latin. The remnants of Brythonic still survive today as Welsh and Breton.

His lifetime saw the downfall of the western Roman empire, in which westwardly migrating peoples such as the Vandals, Goths, Franks and Huns looking for new lands to inhabit (or simply loot) played a major role. There was colossal disorder and unrest, and constant warfare in this period. Rome was sacked by the Goths in 410, and Britain abandoned by the Romans at about the same time. Roman generals tried to resist the tide of new bodies sweeping across their 'civilized' world - Gaul (now France), Italy, Spain, even Greece and north Africa along with Dacia, Dalmatia and other long forgotten provinces. Sometimes they gave these newcomers lands and made them federates of the empire, sometimes they turned them loose upon one other, sometimes they made treaties with them as equals, and sometimes they led the fighting against them. There was no single solution, but for all the Roman resourcefulness, the 'barbarians' took control. However, in occasional pockets of the empire there was strenuous resistance against the newcomers with more than temporary success. These regions included Britain and Brittany.

The figure of Arthur looms large in Western culture through the influence of story-tellers both oral and literary in the course of the Middle Ages. His fame is not commensurate with his importance in the times in which he lived. But somehow he caught the imagination of a group of peoples who had seen one of their own bring success to them at a time when it was far from expected. This success was military, and through his military success came peace, though it was not to last much more than a couple of generations. Other stories also accrued to his name - such stories as of the love of Tristan and Isolde, of the wizard Merlin, and of the mysterious artefact, the Holy Grail.

For centuries tales were told of him and his knights and their adventures, inspiring a number of literary masterpieces throughout Europe. The greatest of these in English is Sir Thomas Malory's *Morte D'Arthur*,[*] written over many years by a man held prisoner for serious crimes at the end of the 15th century. Malory's work is a wonderful summation of the Arthurian literary tradition, combining mainly French romances into a connected whole. It may also be thought of as one of the earliest 'modern' works, written in a language that broadly speaking, we can still understand today, as, for instance, one would not choose to say of earlier writers like Gower and Chaucer.

The world of Malory is a storyteller's world, but this does not mean that we cannot look for certain clues to the original historical background. One of the most important sets of clues is in the *names* - of places certainly but primarily of people.

For instance, near the beginning of Book I, we discover three Romans, Ladinas, Grastian and Placidas (Latinus (?))[†], Gratianus and Placidus.) These men are

---

[*] If we except the small perfection of *Sir Gawain and the Green Knight*.

[†] The Latinus grave stone at Camelford bears witness to the contemporary use of the name.

guarding castles in Gaul 'for dread of king Claudas.' This king probably has his origin in one of the 5th century Frankish kings, most probably Chlodio or Chlodoveus (Clovis). Another of the Franks is found in book VIII, king Faramon, who is clearly Pharamond (died C.430). He is put into the story of Tristan, a 6th century figure as we know from other sources, so we must accept the limits of historical reliability in these romances.

Here are a number of further examples:
1) Anguissance of Ireland may be the Aengus 'ri Alban' king in Britain, known from Irish sources, whose kingdom was on the Plain of Derwent - a location posited by John Morris as most likely to be around the Devon Dart in Dumnonia, where 5th and 6th century Irish inscriptions have been found.
2) Pellinor may be map or ap Eleanor, son of Eleanor (or Leonora), and of Arthur too.
3) King Cradelmas or Cradelment is Cerdic of Elmet, a British kingdom, now part of modern-day Yorkshire.
4) Cador of Cornwall is Cadwy king of Dumnonia datable to the late 5th/ early 6th century.
5) Three more Romans: Florence, Floridas, Phariaunce = Florentius, Floridus, Varianus.
6) Bagdemagus and his son Meliagraunce are perhaps no more than a doublet for Maelwys son of Baeddan in the early Welsh tale *Culhwch and Olwen*, and to be identified with Melvas, a king in Somerset (part of Dumnonia), who in one old story abducts Arthur's wife - or even with the adventurers Bieda and Maegla, who according to the A-S Chronicle came ashore at Portsmouth in 501.
7) Terrabil, the second fortress of Arthur's father - varied from Geoffrey of Monmouth's Castle Dimilioc

- is an old name for Launceston castle,* presumably recorded in the religious quotation encircling the church O quam terribilis….. est locus iste.' The name is probably derived from its massive defences which earned its nickname: Castle Terrible, but, if there were an earlier fortification pre-dating the Norman castle, it might be Ty - or Tre - Riwal.

8) The country of Constantine beside Brittany where Arthur defeats a giant who has been ravaging the countryside is the western coastal district of Normandy known as the Côtentin. This was still recorded as Constantine in the 17th century. But the caveat here is that the Norman rulers were much involved in this part of France, their homeland, and this may have reference to a mediaeval event. Henry I owned the Côtentin shortly after his father's death in 1087. He died shortly before Geoffrey completed his book.

9) Lastly, Lucan the butler (or, Luca the botteler or Lucanere) - and perhaps Lucas as well - may have his prototype in Lucas, the butler of Henry II, who was given the manor of Teignweek in Devon in the latter part of the 12th century for his services. Some wag perhaps displaced Bedivere from his traditional role in favour of the contemporary figure.

What I am proposing is a level of somewhat vague historical reality as a setting for the Arthurian stories in Malory's compendium of romances. There are Romans but not many, there are dark-age kings and adventurers who may well be part of the immediate post-Roman period in Britain: nothing really conclusive, because

---

* As recorded in Carew's Survey. It is spelt *Terrible*.

foreign opponents are mainly lacking; no identifiable Saxons nor Picts, and no later enemies such as Danes or Vikings.* For the most part it is the British amongst themselves unencumbered by outsiders.

The explanation is, I think, a simple one. The stories are set in a time when the British ruled themselves, when they had freedom and control over their own destiny.

Substantially, they lost this from A.D. 43 when the Romans began their conquest. And it was returned to them in the early years of the 5th century, though their territory soon diminished and kept diminishing.

Arthur became the focus of a dream. The dream was autonomy, and, long after autonomy was substantially gone, they could cling to memories of a time when things were different and better.†

But, in making Arthur their focus, they altered him. There must be no limit to his grandeur, to his omnipotence, to his royalty. After Geoffrey of Monmouth, there wasn't much limit to his territory either.

The romantic splendour hid of course ordinary realities: there is no suggestion he was a king till hundreds of years after his death.‡ And if he was, what of?§ He is

---

* Though Malory sometimes appears to introduce mediaeval characters and events, especially from his own time: for instance, Uther's final battle at St Alban's seems to be 15th Century in origin.

† I fear I am guilty of overstatement, for, while Geoffrey of Monmouth had an agenda, *most* storytellers would simply be trying to tell a good story.

‡ Life of Gouéznou, 1019; the contents list to the Historia Brittonum is of uncertain date, but different from the text in naming him as king. It should be highlighted as a separate work e.g. note the number of islands in cap. 67 or the site of Carausius' memorial arch (cap. 24).

§ He could have been a successor to his mother's father, a king, but we don't know where his kingdom was.

constantly described as a leader, and a soldier. A general he was surely, but also a warlord with a formidable private army. A powerful man who must have consorted with kings, he did not necessarily have much success off the battlefield. We do not know.

So, attempting these broad outlines of his life, I speak as I find, with what little particles of evidence I have mustered. Are they wholly convincing? Probably not. But I should wager any amount that some of them are true.

Our first reference to Arthur is from about a century after his death when a British poet Aneirin describes the deeds of another warrior - one of a small cavalry force some 300 strong, who went south from Edinburgh into Yorkshire on a disastrous raid. The poet says how Gwawrddur 'glutted (?) black ravens on the rampant of the stronghold, though he was no Arthur.' This comparison shows that Arthur already has a semi-legendary status as a great fighter, if we believe this text was in Aneirin's original manuscript; which some doubt, but not perhaps with good reason. The earliest copy is mediaeval and has been subject to a few interpolations. I cannot support Thomas Green's idea (see *Postscript*) that Gwawrddur is being compared to a mythological Defender or Protector of Britain.

Sometime in the early 9th century the fascinating compilation known as the Historia Brittonum was put together from a variety of earlier documents: there are possibly fragmentary materials drawn direct from the Arthurian period. What appears to be one of these is justly renowned. It is a battle-list of Arthur's that scholars are inclined to believe is a translation (into Latin prose) of an original British poem; this may be from Arthur's own lifetime. It is so important that I give the full text in chapter 11.

This provides the strongest evidence for Arthur's

British successes and in a preamble we are even given an approximate time-frame. It is easy to scoff and be dismissive because this list is being recorded more than 300 years after Arthur's lifetime. But it would be a brave man who did not acknowledge this as a probable proof of the reality of Arthur's achievements. A couple of other mentions, of a more legendary kind, do nothing to undermine this factual account.

Arthur's concluding battle, the siege of Mount Badon, is happily mentioned by an earlier authority, the monk Gildas C.520, also as a conclusive battle, but he fails to mention who won it.

The great 8th century English historian the Venerable Bede is short of original sources for the Arthurian period and relies heavily on Gildas. However he makes one important mistake by following Gildas too faithfully and placing the coming of the Saxons *after* an important letter datable to 446. They had come to Britain in 428, and the letter is almost certainly *a response to their presence*, a desperate message of appeal for Roman help.

So the traditional chronology has to be revised in the light of this; it has caused no end of confusion for historians, especially as the important Anglo-Saxon Chronicle C.900 follows Bede's mistaken chronology.[*]

Neither Bede nor the A-S Chronicle, while having much interesting information on English matters, knows of Arthur. And it is left to the compiler of some 10th century Welsh annals, the Annales Cambriae, to provide dates for Mount Badon and for Arthur's final battle. These dates are even more flawed than Bede's and the A-S Chronicle's providing another stumbling-block to the

---

[*] I have silently subtracted 21 years from all the early Kentish entries down to 488, for Bede places the Saxon arrival in 449.

truth.

The charming primitive Welsh romance of *Culhwch and Olwen* may belong to the next century. Here Arthur is already in legendary guise, performing heroic and miraculous deeds. In such details as the names of his followers or his court in Cornwall, we may dimly touch historical reality. Finally, there is Geoffrey of Monmouth, the cleric and writer who gave Arthur international fame without letting a good story be too much troubled by a concern for the truth. He completed at the beginning of the reign of King Stephen (1135 - 1154) his 'History of the Kings of Britain'.

His claim to be using an ancient book on British history received from his friend Walter Archdeacon of Oxford may be true - a book which he says was brought out of Brittany. But his additional claim to have translated it from British to Latin without embellishment is much less convincing. In the life of the Breton saint Goueznou written in 1019, we may have another reference to this book.

What is easier to say is that Geoffrey used what early sources he could find - including both Gildas' De Excidio and the Historia Brittonum.[*] He also used his imagination. We take Geoffrey's words literally at our peril: the crowning centrepiece of his book is Arthur who becomes emperor after a pitched battle with the Romans in Gaul (France).

Geoffrey's work preceded by a few years, and largely spawned, the immense quantity of mediaeval romances through a number of European countries. Though some of these are of outstanding merit, they hardly concern the present work, the stream, so to speak, being too much

---

[*] He also claims that the well-informed Walter was himself a source.

muddied from the source. Geoffrey's work becomes a kind of taint on too many literary and historical works that follow, reducing their value for our purposes, such is his cultural dominance. Arthurian writings post-Geoffrey must be used guardedly. Even around his own time, capable historians complained of his work, sometimes in veiled terms.

The historical Arthur can be traced back to a readily defined period after the Romans had abandoned Britain to its fate at the beginning of the 5th century. This was, as already indicated, a tumultuous time in the Western Roman Empire involving the migration of many tribes and peoples westward, some for a place to live having lost their own homes, some with more sinister intentions. To some extent, the peaceful and aggressive intents of those groups were interchangeable.

There is no evidence of Arthur's part in the first post-Roman British generation's defence of their land, to which other names are attached. Arthur seems to have arrived later, and (I believe) his public life straddles the second half of the century, more or less. But what I also believe is that much of his time was spent in northern Gaul, and that he moved between the post-Roman world of Britain and the twilight of the empire where Roman law and bureaucracy, taxation and control persisted. The enemies fighting against whom he earned his reputation included not only Picts and Scots and Saxons but, on another stage, Goths and Franks and even perhaps Huns, where he might have been battling beside Romans. Though the traces of his presence in Gaul are very slight, I have no qualms about proposing this other dimension to his life and career. Perhaps there is still further evidence to be found.

Lastly, I might add that this book is an essay in biography, an attempt to identify Arthur in an historical context. This context is a backdrop, and I hope my book is sooner judged for throwing light on Arthur than the period in which he lived. Not very much is really known about him - some might say, nothing at all - but I am trying here to open up a subject too long largely neglected: are there any truths, are there any *facts* about the legendary hero?

Chapter 1 - How Books Get Written

A terrible event occurred at Glastonbury in the South-West of Britain about the year 520 AD. It would seem that the widow of the recently deceased King Cadwy - he had ruled over the south-westerly province, Dumnonia for many years - had been staying in the famous abbey with her two sons. They had gone into a chapel to pray. Through a side-door had appeared the abbot as if to officiate, but... suddenly turning, he revealed himself as Cadwy's younger brother, Constantine, the regent, dressed in the abbot's robes. In the most shocking manner, before his sister-in-law's horrified gaze he proceeded with the help of other armed men to murder his helpless nephews and the retainers who tried to protect them. Their blood stained the altar - perhaps the self-same altar before which earlier in the year Constantine had sworn his oath as regent to do no harm to his subjects.

The sole survivor, the distraught and broken-hearted queen sent a letter to one of the leading churchmen of the time recounting the ghastly incident with bitter complaints and lamentations. And for this man, already appalled by the immorality and lawlessness of contemporary life, that was to be the final straw. He set pen to paper to give his unsparing views both on the dismal past of the Britons and the present climate of immorality[1]. It is from this man - Gildas - that we learn of the murders, for his work has fortunately survived. And here we find ourselves so tantalizingly close to the object of our search, for the dead king had been no less than Arthur's own good friend.

Throughout his book Gildas never names Arthur, but he tells us one very significant fact about himself: that he was born in the year of the siege of Mount Badon.* And we have reason to believe that this was Arthur's greatest and certainly most important success. So here is a big chronological clue placing Arthur roughly two generations before Gildas. Arthur's final battle (in which, or, as a result of which he died) is given in another early source as occurring 21 years after Badon. So Gildas was about 21 at the time of Arthur's death. Gildas lived a long and successful life, dying in 570. We are almost certainly correct in placing his birth and Badon in the period 475-500, and Arthur's death in the period 495-520, though Gildas writes of a long vanished time when British success had been achieved, suggesting to us an early date for these battles, close to 475 for Badon, and close to 495 for his death.

Gildas' words are these, describing the events that followed Badon when he was growing up: 'But not even now as formerly are the cities of our country inhabited. But to the present they lie deserted, in ruins and squalor. For our wars may have ceased with foreigners, but not with one another. For the memory of so hopeless a collapse of the island and its unlooked for rescue stuck in the minds of those who witnessed both extraordinary events. And for this reason kings, public and private persons, priests and clergy fulfilled each their function. But these dying, when a generation had succeeded that was ignorant of that great convulsion and only aware of the present calm, so all controls of truth and justice were shaken and subverted, and not even a memory, let alone a trace, can be found in the aforementioned ranks, a few

---

* Gildas gives no indication where he is residing at the time of his book. Though conceivably Ireland, this is most likely the north.

only excepted…'

Chapter 2 - Arthur's beginnings

It was about 100 years before those words were written that Arthur was born. There is no record of his actual date of birth, but I believe it is possible to show that he was born close to the year 425.

Geoffrey of Monmouth is our earliest source for his birth, and since he wrote more than 700 years later it is of course easy to look askance at his version of events.

He tells us that an aristocrat of Dumnonia, the most south-westerly province of Britain, living in what is now north Cornwall, was married to Igerna (Eigr) whom we know from other sources to have been daughter of a king, presumably of some province of Southern Britain and perhaps of Dumnonia itself, whose name was Anblaud.

Her husband, duke Gorlois or Gorlwys was master of a fortress or secure place on the northern coast and another one further inland. These were called Tintagel and Dimilioc respectively, sites still known today.

At Tintagel we know there was a fortress dating from Norman times, but we have no proof of earlier fortification, though there was a dark-age population of some sort. Recent archaeological evidence suggests it was residence to someone of high status.

Geoffrey describes Tintagel in these terms: 'The castle is built high above the sea, which surrounds it on all sides, and there is no other way in except that offered by a narrow isthmus of rock. Three armed soldiers could hold it against you, even if you stood there with the whole kingdom of Britain at your side.' This remarkable description of the medieval castle's impregnability is borne out by our knowledge of the little causeway that undoubtedly once existed, and might suggest Gorlwys' importance.[*]

But Geoffrey's attempt to aggrandize Arthur's origins leads him into a dubious fantasy about the king of Britain, allegedly Uther Pendragon,[†] conceiving a passion for Igerna, and going to war against Gorlwys whom he kills before seducing Igerna and fathering Arthur.

Uther Pendragon is a shadowy figure outside the pages of Geoffrey - perhaps a ruler in the north of Britain. Geoffrey's story of the passion and the killing, however, is curiously reminiscent of an event recorded by tradition from 10th century English history.

Edgar, king of England, heard rumours of the beauty of Aelfthryth (Elfrida) daughter of the earl of Devon (also in Dumnonia). He sent down a trusted courtier Ethelwold to find out if the rumours were true.

Although the rumours *were* true, Ethelwold wanted her for himself. So he lied to Edgar and married her. But, the rumour persisting, Edgar came down to Devon to see for himself. He fell in love with her too. First, the king eliminated his rival - with a javelin thrust while out hunting. Then in 965 he and Aelfthryth were married. Surely Geoffrey knew this story!

So I doubt very much that Gorlwys, whose name is perhaps commemorated in a camp named Carhurles on the edge of Bodmin moor, had anything to do with a King Uther.[‡] But it seems likely that Gorlwys died not long after

---

[*] There is still access to the 'island' by a modern path.

[†] The theory that an expression meaning 'terrible boy' was misunderstood as 'son of Uther' is of interest. A mediaeval gloss is its origin.

[‡] But it must be stated that in the Dialogue of Arthur and the Eagle dating to the 12th century and seeming to incorporate traditions pre-Geoffrey, Uther's son and grandson are named as Arthur's brother and nephew. Dare

Arthur's birth. For this might explain why Arthur was sent away as a child. At any rate, Igerna's (second?) husband is recorded as Rica, chief elder of Cornwall, his son Gormant being described as Arthur's brother on his mother's side.

---

one suggest that Uther was Igerna's husband *before* Gorlwys?

Another obscure poem of an uncertain date, Uther Pendragon's Elegy, also appears to link Uther with Arthur. One line can be read as Uther's pride in his son. My feeling would be that Geoffrey's linkage of Arthur with Uther has been connected in these poems with existing knowledge about Uther. (Geoffrey indicates no awareness of Arthur's linkage with Anbland.)

Chapter 3 - Arthur, Cei, and Bedwyr

Gorlwys was dead by about 430, and, not long after, Arthur's mother (and step-father?) made the decision to send him to relatives in Wales. We do not know why. There is no special reason to think that either the raids of Picts and Scots or the (probably subsequent) break-out and subsequent warfare of the Germanic federates in the South-East would have had any particular impact on peaceful, sea-locked Dumnonia. Perhaps the young Arthur made the request to go himself. There is also that common tradition by which step-parents neglect or maltreat children not their own, but the more likely with the step-mother.

The head of the household to whom he was sent was named Kenyr Keinuarvawc or Kenyr the fair-bearded. Since tradition connects his son with Caer Gai (in the parish of Llanuwchllyn) in Bala and two early poets give the alternative name of Caer Gynyr (derived from his own name), this is probably where he lived.

Of this man a single piece of information is vouchsafed us in one of the old Triads,[*] as follows:

Kynyr or Kevyr (by another name) and Meilir and Yneigr, sons of Gwron ap Cunedda, who were all three with Cadwallon Lawhir their cousin when he drove the Gwyddyl Ffichti from Môn. And then they destroyed them (the Gwyddyl Ffichti) completely, when Cadwallon Lawhir slew Seregri Wyddel (the Irishman) in Llan y Gwyddyl at Caer Gybi (Holyhead) in Môn.

So a settlement of Irishmen on Anglesey was wiped out by warrior Britons in the mid years of the 5th century.

---

[*] See Bromwich p. 258.

But what is interesting from our point of view may be expressed in the form of a genealogy.

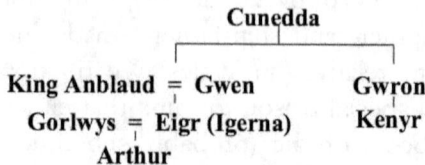

Igerna's mother and Kenyr's father were sister and brother, by descent from a famous northern chieftain who settled in Wales as a mercenary.* Arthur was travelling to his mother's first cousin, his own great-uncle's son[2].

The mediaeval romances make out that Arthur was fostered by the wife of a lord whose name is given as Ector. If we see in this name a truncated version of a Roman title - most probably "Protector" which was used by another British king Vortiporius within the century following, then again we can return to Kenyr, for the romances concur with Welsh tradition that Kenyr/Ector's son was called Cei (Kay).

Thus began a great friendship between these two, Cei and Arthur, and in these parts also, growing up beside lovely Bala Lake, we may suppose they found the third intimate of their little circle, Bedwyr (Bedivere), the son of Bedrawc or Pedrawc. The trio were to be inseparable.

But there are no stories of Arthur's childhood. The charming romance story of his pulling the sword from the stone prior to his coronation - not found in Geoffrey's

---

* I differ from John Morris' and others' chronology here, placing Cunedda's arrival in Maximus' time or slightly later; and the Irishmen's expulsion between 430 and 460.

version - may well be based on a legendary event in the life of the 11th century St Wulfstan, bishop of Worcester. He is supposed to have been asked for his pastoral staff by William the Conqueror who wanted him out. But he took it to the marble tomb of Edward the Confessor by whom the bishopric had been conferred, declaring, "Take it, my lord king, and give it to whomever you will," as he struck the staff upon the tomb. The marble opened to receive it nor could anyone be found to remove it until he had been reinstated.

The next event in Arthur's life must surely date from the late 430s/ early 440s. But it finds its earliest record about 1190, in what is known as the Vulgate Cycle of romances: Arthur has a relationship with Lissanor or Lionors, daughter of Count Sevain.* The Count is said to be 'of Canparcorentin'. This is the fortified town of Quimper in Brittany, capital of the ancient kingdom of Cornouaille, associated with the early Celtic saint Corentin who was probably still living at the time.

This brief liaison serves little purpose in the narrative, though the same source gives the couple a son, Loholt. Isn't it possible that such a relationship really did occur - and where more likely for their involvement than Quimper, the town named in the romance text?†

The connexions between the south-west of Britain and Brittany were strong. We know of instances in this period where wealthy Britons had land on both sides of the water. There was also Arthur's mother's sister

---

* Called earl Sanam by Malory, clearly a corruption of Sevain.

† A Latin locative case, *at Quimper*, may have been misunderstood as a genitive, *of Quimper*. The romancer may have discovered an ancient marriage record.

Rienguleid. She had married a Breton warrior named Bican and gone to live in Brittany. Might Arthur have stayed with her?

But, most interestingly, the name of the young lady's father, Sevain - filtered through the French romances - is exceedingly reminiscent of Sefin, a name recorded in one early Welsh poem as Cei's father. In Rachel Bromwich's words: "It is tempting to see in Sefin>Sevin a corruption of Cenir." I propose that Kenyr and Sevain are one and the same person.

So now Leonora,[*] as I prefer to call her (a name consonant with the period) springs to life as Cei's sister. This short-lived liaison is with a cousin he has known almost all his life. And if Arthur and Leonora are in Quimper at the time of their love affair, probably Cei is also. My own suggestion would be that these young British aristocrats have come for a Gallo-Roman education.

---

[*] Alienor, Eleanor, and perhaps Azenor, are other linked names, it would seem.

Chapter 4 - Britain 383 - 412

While Arthur was growing up in what we may hope was peace and prosperity - though having already experienced his father's death and a degree of separation from his mother - events in Britain were far less rosy.

The collapse of Roman rule in Britain might be dated from the rebellion of a Spanish general in 383 who sought to make himself emperor.[*] Magnus Maximus, supreme Commander of the troops in Britain, who had fought successfully against the marauding Picts and Scots, had five years of adventure with France and Spain under his control before defeat at the hands of Theodosius the Great in 388.

We do not really know how this affected Britain, but many of his troops would have died and others not returned. Legend, which probably here has a substantial degree of reality, says many of his men settled in Brittany.

In 407 another adventurer, with the great name of Constantine, and said to be the son of a Roman senator and a prostitute,[†] set out for the continent to emulate his predecessor. His 4-year adventure also ended in death. If it was a tragedy for him, it was equally for the country he ruled. The skeleton force left behind meant the country was dangerously vulnerable. An old chronicle tells us, for

---

[*] These usurpers often had the position foisted upon them by the rebellious troops under their command: to refuse the imperial role would invite death. So they would make the best of their precarious status.

[†] The Angevin Chronicles. The historians had some doubt whether he came from the lowest background or something rather different. The senator Constantius' obtaining a commission for his illegitimate son in a distant province is curiously modern.

the year 409 or 410: 'The provinces of Britain were devastated by Saxon invasion.' These Germanic intruders not unknown in Britain since at least the middle of the previous century were seizing their chance to exploit the situation. And Britain appears to have been virtually defenceless. Rome was sacked for three days by the Goths about the same time - though the imperial court had already moved to Ravenna. This was a moment with a message: the Western Roman Empire[*] was now unsafe. It may be worth considering how much Constantine's attempt at usurpation had to answer for. For within the western empire he had been the most pressing Roman problem at that time.

With Constantine's failure and death, Britain was a soft target for marauders. As well as marauders by profession - Picts from what is now Scotland, Scots from Ireland who had settled in the north, and the Germanic adventurers, there was also the great and increasing problem of migrant peoples, the origins of whose migrations are obscure. There was a westward drive from the east beginning perhaps in Russia, perhaps due to climate change. Little-known peoples appeared out of the Caucasus and surrounding areas seeking new land, having lost their own. Many were harmless or decent, but, in trying to survive, they encroached on peoples already settled in the west. War was an inevitability when goodwill broke down. The Franks, the Goths, the Vandals, the Huns, the Alans and others tried the patience of the Western empire to its limits. They were collectively

---

[*] The Empire had been divided many years before. The Eastern empire still to last another 1000 years, was based on the ancient Byzantium, later Constantinople, now Istanbul in western Turkey.

thought of as 'barbarians' by the Romans. But historians are apt to look more kindly on them now. Their cultures were different from the Romans', but there is no evidence of greater harshness or cruelty. Indeed it is clear that because of the impositions of Roman taxation and authority, many even in the settled west came to prefer barbarian overlords to their existing Roman ones.

After the Saxon raid the Britons seem themselves to have begun counter-attacking, freeing their cities from barbarian pressure. They are said to have inspired the people of Brittany and other provinces of Gaul to follow their example. A doubtful rescript of about this date seems to suggest that the emperor Honorius had washed his hands of British involvement, presumably having more pressing matters to attend to.[*]

We know little of the years following Constantine's demise. The Anglo-Saxon Chronicle prepared about the time of King Alfred (C.900) has an entry under 418 detailing the departure of the Roman inhabitants from Britain. This entry - from some old lost chronicle, one would imagine - finds its fullest form in the pages of another slightly later 10th century chronicle, one expression being especially worthy of remark: 'The Romans *not enduring the manifold menacing of the tribes...*[†] set

---

[*] It may refer to an Italian province but is most probably concerned with Britain.

[†] Tribes - 'gentes' - does not adequately convey the marauding peoples and this explanation can probably be discounted. (We would have expected an expression such as 'tribes of the barbarians'.) It is the indigenous population being referred to. The quotation is from Ethelwerd. However a remark of the 8th century Paulus Diaconus (XIII.5), relating to the time when the Britons sought help from Honorius, *not enduring the infestation of the Scots and Picts*, ought to receive a mention. The parallelism is undeniable: might Ethelwerd be *borrowing*?

sail for Gaul. etc.' Surely this important passage is our only record of the naked hostility of the indigenous Britons for the Romans.

Perhaps, as we are told in the pages of Gildas, a legion returned once or twice and with great success.* But, despite such surprising interventions, the Britons were now on their own.

---

* See Appendix: The Last Legions in Britain.

Chapter 5 - Britain 425 - 429

'Meanwhile [in the reign of Vortigern] came three keels from Germany driven into exile. In them were the brothers Horsa and Hengest ...'
(Historia Brittonum)

'But Vortigern held power in Britain when Theodosius and Valentinian were consuls [425] and in the 4th year of his reign the Saxons came to Britain ... and were received by Vortigern ...'
(Historia Brittonum)

In the year 425 a man called Vortigern was declared king. There were regional kings all over Britain, so far as we can tell, but this seems to have been a different kind of event - a paramount sovereignty of Britain.

At a guess, one might see the Romans behind this radical step, advising unity and a central government such as they had given to Britain. But it may have been a meeting of the chieftains and extensive lobbying to reach a verdict on what to do as an autonomous country.

Legend suggests that Vortigern was a usurper with no right to this coveted position. But Vortigern fell from British favour, as we shall see, and hindsight may have dictated the negative way in which he was later perceived[3].

What we know suggests he was from a powerful Gloucester dynasty. There were many Roman estates in this part of Britain bordering Wales. And his family may have intermarried with the Romans. Indeed, if a dark-age monument is to be believed, Vortigern had married Severa, the daughter of Magnus Maximus, the Spanish adventurer[4].

Vortigern had urgent problems over the future of the

country. The assaults of the marauding peoples had not ceased. Military training was going to be essential, and soon. But in the midst of his predicament an unusual solution surfaced involving a calculated risk.

While the British were being harassed on all sides by unwanted and dangerous visitors, three boatloads of Saxons arrived in 428 somewhere in the South[*] from the German coast. They had been driven out of their own country -for reasons uncertain - as the Historia Brittonum tells us. We cannot now know their leaders' intentions, but past history - both their own[†] and the Saxons' generally - would suggest they were up to no good.

Probably they picked the wrong landing-point: they were surprised and surrounded. These new arrivals were in trouble. But, in circumstances we do not understand, a deal was struck after they were brought before Britain's leader - a deal which would destroy Vortigern and Britain both, but actually the sensible deal of a man who had Britain's interests at heart and who was doing nothing lightly or foolishly. He would have consulted his 'concilium' or team of advisors,[‡] who probably agreed wholeheartedly to the decision made. But, when things went badly wrong, there was only one scapegoat. It is time to rehabilitate this unlucky man.

The agreement was that they could stay as federates

---

[*] Ypwines fleot has been identified with Ebbsfleet.

[†] See Appendix: Hengest and Hnaef. Gildas, who is followed by Bede and the A-S Chronicle, says they were invited *from Germany*. But the Historia Brittonum account makes more sense.

[‡] Obviously, the nature of the concilium is uncertain. It may have been more like a parliament.

of the British, and be given land and provisions, in return for defending the British against the invading hordes. Both parties were no doubt very happy, though the Saxon devastations of 409/10 were not so far distant, and various intervening raids must have occurred from the same quarter. Hengest their leader perhaps had very winning ways!

This policy of federates may have been another Roman suggestion. But we may imagine the collective sigh of the British establishment. These Saxons numbered only perhaps 200 or 300, but somehow the Britons could feel they were returning the battle to the enemy. They had allies in their struggle.

The Saxon contingent were given the island of Thanet off the coast of Kent in the south-east as their base, not far from London. More good news arrived the following year. A joint attack by Picts and other Saxons was repulsed through the means of a very remarkable Gallic bishop Germanus of Auxerre who happened to be visiting Britain. He had been a military leader, and, galvanizing the British troops in high country close to an unidentified river in southern Britain, he routed the enemy, in part or even largely through the battle cry 'Hallelujah'.[*] God was on Britain's side! But it was not to last.

---

[*] Gildas cap. 20 records this victory - 'trusting not in man but in God'.

Chapter 6 - Britain 430 - 446

The harrowing events of the next decade and a half may be roughly reconstructed from three of our most important sources: Gildas, the Historia Brittonum, and the Anglo-Saxon Chronicle. They do not make for easy reading.

More Saxons arrived 'and the British could not feed them' …..The British said they could not give them food and clothing because of the increase in numbers. They asked them to go away. The Saxon response was to think of ways to break the peace. But Hengest suggested to Vortigern - improbable as it may sound - increasing the number of federates; to which Vortigern is supposed to have agreed. And 16 more boats arrived.[*]

If there is an atom of truth in this, something very important has been omitted. Hengest's daughter - with whom Vortigern soon fell in love - can hardly be the answer. We are simply in the dark. Perhaps a land deal was struck: that in return for services provided free, Vortigern must provide land for everybody, on a much larger scale than little Thanet. This might explain why Vortigern handed Kent over to the Saxons soon after - ignoring the poor British king who ruled there. This seems more realistic than a drunken Vortigern turning to Hengest, having been smitten with the daughter and saying: 'Ask of me what you will, even to the half of my kingdom.' He is afterwards said to have married her.

Vortigern is recorded as agreeing to another huge Saxon force including Hengest's son travelling north

---

[*] Gildas Cap.23.4 notes a second and 'larger troop' of Saxons arriving.

against the Irish (Scoti) settled in Scotland. Their brief did not apparently include interference with the Picts, whom they left alone.* If we remember Germanus' attack on the Pict/Saxon consortium, one would guess at some arrangements between the two peoples - hardly to the advantage of the British.

Gildas paints a horribly gloomy picture of the history of the time and probably offers a *northern* perspective, as his father seems to have been a chieftain or dignitary in Southern Scotland.

He gives us a number of events following the departure of the Romans primarily or almost entirely based upon tradition. This may be outlined as follows:

Cap 19.
1) Renewed attacks of Picts and Scots.
2) Seizure of the north of Britain right up to (Hadrian's) wall.
3) Wall abandoned and neighbouring towns.
4) Massacres of Britons, survivors looting one another; famine.

Cap 20.
5) A desperate letter by the British to the Roman Commander in Gaul. (This can be dated to 446).
6) Further famine.

---

* The A-S Chronicle records Saxon successes against the Picts in the early days of their mercenary status. It is fair to assume Hengest earned his payment for the first four years or so. A friendship may have sprung up between Hengest and a king of Elmet, in the north, at this time. A gloss or variant in the Historia Brittonum records him acting as Hengest's interpreter. Henry of Huntingdon has the Saxons fighting near Stamford in Lincolnshire which may be based on local tradition: Henry lived close by.

7) A fight-back leading to the Hallelujah Victory (429).
8) Decrease of incursions from Picts and Scots.

Cap 21.
9) Sudden, extraordinary abundance 'that no previous age had known anything like it'.
10) Failure of morality.

Cap 22.
11) Rumour of the approach of 'the old enemy'.
12) A deadly plague. (Sometime between 443 and 450).

Cap 23.
13) Saxons invited by the British.
14) Three boats arrive with auguries prophesying 150 years of pillaging Britain (428)
15) Saxons given land and provisions.
16) Threat to break agreement.

Cap 24.
17) Devastation from sea to sea. (452)
18) Terrible British suffering.

We need not doubt that all or most of these events are real, but it's a desperate chronological muddle. Northern traditions seem intermingled with wrongly placed but datable events. Gildas has done his best, but his summary is a hopeless failure. Nevertheless he remains our only source for the famines, and the abundance, the Saxon prophecy, the plague and the 446 letter - however confused we may find ourselves.

The Historia Brittonum and Anglo-Saxon Chronicle give

us a clearer understanding. The first serious Saxon breakout took place in about 433* or 434, on the Kentish river Darent. The British were led by an able leader, Vortimer, Vortigern's son. The following year, at a site identified with Aylesford in Kent, Vortimer fought with Hengest again. The brother of each of them was said to have been killed in the battle.†

A third battle gave a great victory to the Britons by the Inscribed Stone, a long vanished Roman monument on the coast. 'They [the Saxons] fled to their keels and were drowned as they clambered aboard them like women.'

But during this fluctuating warfare in which Vortimer on three occasions enclosed the Saxons in Thanet, effectively rescuing Kent, the Saxons kept appealing for help from their own provinces. And their compatriots came.

In a disastrous battle in 435, Hengest defeated the Britons at Crayford in Kent. Four companies of or 4000 British soldiers were wiped out. 'And the Britons then forsook Kent and fled to London in great terror'. The battle for Kent was lost, and the Saxons were here to stay. In this battle, or more probably shortly before, Vortimer died.

Sometime after the battle of Crayford, Hengest

---

* This was following a treaty between the Saxons and the Picts, according to Bede.

† Alleged burial sites for one or both brothers nearby -at a cromlech called Kit's Coty House, and at Horsted- must be considered uncertain, though the tradition goes back to Bede who says there was a monument in eastern Kent bearing Horsa's (Hengest's supposed brother's) name. This is the best evidence for Horsa's existence, but not conclusive.

instigated peace terms, requesting a permanent treaty. His position was very strong and Vortigern was said to be the Saxons' friend by virtue of his marriage.

Vortigern called a council of his elders. All were for peace. It was agreed that the two sides should meet unarmed to confirm the treaty.

Having arrived at the site of the conference and taken their seats by their supposed new friends, the Britons were set upon and murdered by the Saxons who had knives concealed in their shoes.

Hengest had given the signal for the attack. Only Vortigern was spared, for the purpose of ransom. Land was subsequently transferred to the Saxons in return for Vortigern's life. The Historia Brittonum says the transfer included Essex and Sussex, but this is not credible.

If one doubts the Saxons' horrendous act of treachery in which 300 are said to have died, one might recall in recent times the IRA attempts to destroy the British Cabinet and, in a separate incident, the Tory high command in Brighton. Guy Fawkes and many others litter world history with similar enterprises, sometimes successful. The silence of the Anglo-Saxon Chronicle is no more than we should expect.

In the year 436 - possibly as a direct consequence of the massacre of the Council -more fighting took place at an unidentified site named Guoloppum, probably one of the Wallops in Hampshire.* The two protagonists are named as Vitalinus and Ambrosius. We have genealogical evidence demonstrating that Vitalinus was very probably a member of Vortigern's family, if not Vortigern himself.

---

* There are Wallops also east of Welshpool, in the old Montgomeryshire that is connected with Ogyrfan. (See cap. 10).

For people in this period have not only multiple names - both Roman and British - but also titles. 'Vortigern' - great lord - may have been one such title. But at any rate we are seeing Ambrosius squaring up to a senior British figure. We know that Vortigern was afraid of this man.

Most probably he was a young Roman, perhaps related to the great Christian leader, bishop Ambrose (Aurelius Ambrosius) of Milan who dominated the imperial court at the end of the previous century.

Gildas tells us that this young man's full name was Ambrosius Aurelianus and holds him in reverence - praise in general coming very sparingly from Gildas' pen. Gildas tells us that the Britons took up arms under his leadership and began a fight-back.

Certainly a void might have been left by the deaths of Vortimer and his brother (both of whom Gildas fails to mention); but this 'battle' which seems to have been no more than a skirmish looks like a significant political event: a Romano-British leader, after heavy arguing with a British counterpart, goes it alone, no longer accountable to the British leadership which he despises. A number of Britons and the remaining Romans followed him, one would guess. There were to be no more treaties, no more peace talks, no more leaning on dubious allies and federates. War was the order of the day until their enemies were contained or expelled. So began, I believe, what became known as the 44 years' war.

We have a little information on the first decade of the war. A 5th century Gallic Chronicle and another scarcely later in date concur gloomily on British disaster. The earlier chronicle runs, for 441-2: 'The provinces of Britain up to this time exercised by various disasters and misfortunes are reduced into the power of the Saxons.'

It is difficult to make sense of such a statement

except with reference to the South-East. Had London been taken by the Saxons? The only Anglo-Saxon entry for this period tells of a battle in 444 at Wippedsfleet - which does not seem to have been a Saxon victory. Both sides' successes are unrecorded. But there is no escaping the British despair in the letter sent to the Gallic supreme commander in 446 of which a little has been preserved by Gildas.

It began: 'To Aetius three times consul, the groans of the Britons'. And further on they wrote: 'The barbarians push us back to the sea, the sea pushes us back to the barbarians; between these two kinds of death we face drowning or murder'. Gildas tells us there was no military response to this.[*]

Desperate times! But this is surely written by those who lived not far from Kent and not far from the coast. The Saxons were driving forward implacably.

---

[*] See Appendix 5: The Letter to Aetius.

Chapter 7 - The Continental Picture

We left Arthur in Quimper with his girlfriend Leonora and her brother Cei. The time is the early 440s, they having first arrived perhaps in the previous decade. I suggested they were enjoying a Gallo-Roman education.

Arthur's cousin Illtud must have had such an education if we are to believe the earliest biographical sketch of him by a Breton monk: '….This Illtud was a disciple of St Germanus and St Germanus himself had ordained him priest in his youth….. In truth Illtud was of all Britons the most accomplished in all the scriptures…. and in those of every kind of philosophy viz, geometry, rhetoric, grammar and arithmetic and all the theories of philosophy. And by birth he was a wise magician, having knowledge of the future….'[*]

It is quite possible that the boy Illtud, born in the mid-430s, had studied briefly under Germanus who had marked him out for the priesthood. Perhaps his cousin Arthur studied under Germanus too, but at any rate by c.444 Germanus was dead.

In Gaul and throughout the Western Roman Empire one charismatic leader had shone pre-eminent almost from the time of Arthur's birth. His name was Flavius Aetius. A native of Moesia on the lower Danube, he had been in his youth a hostage both with the Goths and the Huns. (His father was also a general). He married a Goth. By the death of the emperor Honorius in 423 he was already a powerful figure, having the backing of the Huns with whom he was on friendly terms. In the time of the

---

[*] This account is from the 7th century Life of St. Samson of Dol who studied under Illtud.

next emperor, Valentinian III he won favour with him and Valentinian's mother, the formidable Placidia. By the time he had supplanted Placidia's preferred choice, the general Felix as master of the soldiers in 429 - he had him executed the following year - this man had no rivals. His broad shoulders supported the destiny of the western empire until his death, many years after. It was said of him: 'To put it briefly, he... wielded the greatest power such that not only kings but even nations dwelling nearby came at his orders'.*

From our perspective, it was his responsibility to manage peoples residing in Gaul. These were the indigenous tribes including, in the north-west, the Armoricans; the Gallo-Romans; the Goths and Franks, from amongst the new hordes of immigrants; there had been other foreigners such as Vandals, Alans and Suevians in the time of Constantine the British usurper, and it is an intriguing argument that Constantine had crossed the channel into Gaul, at least in part to protect Britain from incursions by these new groups. At the time of his death Germanus was trying to protect the Armoricans from Alans who had been sent in against them by Aetius as a punishment for their perceived arrogance.†

There were also the Burgundians, a Germanic people with whom Aetius‡ had great difficulties before their loyalty to the empire was established. All in all, a hugely volatile situation where the next flare-up was not always easy to predict; and often where a balancing out of power

---

* John of Antioch.

† Aetius probably feared another outbreak of the Bacaudae. (See later)

‡ With an army of Huns he killed their king and 20,000 of them in 435.

needed to be fought for, to prevent the dominance of any one group - unless it were the Gallo-Romans themselves!

In the vast area called the Armorican tract in the north-west - much larger than present-day Brittany and extending south to the river Loire - lived along with the Armoricans and Gallo-Romans two other significant groups.

One was the émigrés from Britain. When they started coming, we do not really know. I have said before that connexions were close enough for a number of wealthy Britons - especially of the south-west - to have property in this region.

At the end of the 4th century and beginning of the 5th it is very likely that there was an active British emigration, in addition to the possibility of Maximus' and Constantine's troops returning there. The stark words of the Historia Brittonum read: '... After the killing of the tyrant Maximus (i.e. 388)... for 40 years they (the Britons) went in fear.'

Lastly, there were the Bacaudae. These can be understood as 'The Travelling Bands'. They would seem to have been displaced and dispossessed inhabitants and others who could not cope with the exorbitant Roman tax system; people of a nomadic disposition probably also joined them; and slaves.

These poor people were seen as a grave threat to the stability of empire. There was no peace for these gypsies of the road. And we may suppose they were treated as a dangerous sub-class, unable to establish any territory for themselves even if they had wanted to. They were known of from as early as the 3rd century.

In 435, 'Western Gaul followed Tibatto chief in the revolt and withdrew from Roman society... almost all the slaves (or, serfs) of Gaul conspired in a Bacauda.' And, in

437, 'Tibatto was captured and the other heads of the rebellion were partly defeated, partly slaughtered, and so the Bacaudan uproar quietened down'. So they 'withdrew'. But the authorities did not wish to let them go. And confrontation and murder brought their separation to an end.

Here was the world the young British aristocrat moved in, not only amongst family and friends of his own background and the educated Gallo-Romans from his own class, but overlapping with Armoricans, Roman ex-soldiers, occasional foreigners of all sorts, and members of the 'travelling bands' when they showed their faces. A cosmopolitan and culturally vibrant world, in which a sensible man might be intrigued far more than frightened by the unknown peoples from the east.

Chapter 8 - The Continent → 451

An agreement for peace seems to have been reached between the Armoricans and the Alans in the early or mid 440s. How far this would have impacted on the Gallo-Romans, Britons and others in Brittany we cannot be sure, but probably not very much.

Other problems in the region equally pressing took the form of the Goths and the Franks, Germanic peoples - the first traceable to Southern Scandinavia in the 1st century, the second a tribal coalition dating from the 3rd century when they were living in the lower and middle Rhine. A branch of the Goths known as the Visigoths were driven across the lower Danube by the Huns in 376. After the memorable victory at Adrianople in 378 in which the emperor Valens was killed, they had spells as federates and marauders alternately. In 410, under their leader Alaric, they sacked Rome after devastating Greece and parts of Italy. And by 418 they were settled in Spain and in Gaul between the mouths of the Garonne and the Loire with Toulouse as their capital.

The emperor Julian had granted a large area of land, Toxandria near the Rhine, to a branch of the Franks, the Salians after a violent outbreak in 335. But in 425 the Salians abandoned their home, and the Franks of the middle Rhine also crossed into Gaul. Many of Aetius' efforts were directed against these two Frankish groups in trying to prevent their passage south and west.

A great battle was fought at an unknown site Vicus Helena C.440 or a little later in which Aetius defeated the Franks under their king Chlodio,* perhaps somewhere

---

* The usual transliteration with or without the 'h' of 'Chlogio', as given by Sidonius and Gregory of Tours. The form *Chlodio* is also found.

around the Pas-de-Paris in the north-east.* But there must have been many other encounters. The 6th century historian Gregory of Tours has left us this note on Chlodio: 'They... say that Chlodio, a man of high birth and marked ability among his people, was King of the Franks and that he lived in the castle of Duisburg in Thuringian territory.... Chlodio sent spies to the town of Cambrai. When they had discovered all that they needed to know, he himself followed and crushed the Romans and captured the town. He lived there only a short time and then occupied the country up to the river Somme. Some say that Merovech, the father of Childeric, was descended from Chlodio.' Having succeeded as it would seem to the throne of the semi-legendary Pharamond, Chlodio ruled from C.431 to C. 449.†

Turning now from authentic history to early accounts of Arthur's own career as a warrior, we are pleased to note the sources that place him campaigning in Gaul. One of these is Geoffrey, and the other about a century earlier. I shall quote the passage in the earlier source, the Life of Goueznou (a Breton saint). A priest called William, chaplain to Bishop Eudo of Léon, dedicated the work to his superior in 1019.

---

* Favoured sites include Vieil-Hesdin, Lens and, especially, Hélesmes.

† In consequence of a power struggle after his death, one of Chlodio's sons, an adolescent with immensely long fair hair - the length being a ritualized part of royal tradition - was adopted by Aetius. The young man's brother Merovech, the next king, must have been considerably older, by at least 15 years, and probably in fact a half-brother; this would go some way towards accounting for the dynasty's subsequent name: Merovingian. Tradition doubted that he was Chlodio's son at all (see Cap. 15). The historian Priscus had seen the younger of these brothers at Rome. He was called Aetius.

He tells in a preface how Conan Meriadoc settled in Brittany after having conquered one of the 'lesser kingdoms', and then slaughtering the native Armoricans in the newly conquered regions: the Britons and Armoricans 'under the same laws and bound by fraternal (!) treaties' began to live as one people.

'Sometime after' (he continues), 'Vortigern became king by usurpation', and he repeats the story of Vortigern's fateful invitation to the Saxons. But, after much bloodshed...

'The pride of these Saxons was later controlled by the great Arthur king of the Britons, and they were driven out of most of the island and forced into slavery. But when that same Arthur, after many glorious victories won in British and Gallic fields of theatre was called at last from worldly activity, the way was clear once more for those Saxons who had remained in the island...'

William cites British - or, Breton - history as his authority. But he may mean a book called 'The British (or, Breton) History'. Geoffrey claims possession of a similar very old book obtained from his good friend Walter Archdeacon of Oxford, Provost of St George's College: it had been brought out of Brittany. It is very possible the book therefore did exist, but we must admit the convenience of Geoffrey's claim to a unique source. At least we can probably be confident that Geoffrey had some little known historical materials to draw upon - however hard it is to distinguish them from Geoffrey's 'creative' use of them (including a degree of wild synthesizing).

Geoffrey takes Arthur into Gaul twice, first to confront a Roman tribune, and the second time to take on the full might of the Roman empire in a great war with the procurator, representative of the emperor.

In the first episode, Arthur crosses over from Britain and lands in Gaul, laying waste the countryside. The tribune Flollo[*] then ruling Gaul comes out with his forces to meet him and is defeated in battle. Flollo flees to Paris and Arthur besieges him there. Finally Flollo offers Arthur single combat to decide the outcome, and Arthur agrees. He is victorious, and Paris with Flollo's troops throws open its gates and surrenders to him.

This story is worth little in terms of history. The Romans were not at enmity with Britons or Bretons. Nor is there any known leader Flollo (who is said to rule in the name of the emperor Leo).

However, this very odd name - sometimes varied to the easier 'Frollo' - may repay study. Here is the Breton scholar Léon Fleuriot, talking about a Frankish king, Childebert: 'We have noted the variants Philibert in the lives of saint Paul and saint Malo, Hylibert in the Cartulary of Landévennec. The name of Childebert (Xildebert) in the 6th century has undergone two different developments: initial X sometimes becomes f, as in Chlodobert > Flobert, sometimes h - (in Hylibert) as in Chlodowig > Hlodowig.' For example in the British Annals of St Neots, perhaps of the early 12th century - here derived from Norman annals (Annales Uticenses) - we find the beginning of Clovis II's reign to have been marked as of Flodoveus (Chlodoveus).[†]

Again we find that from the Roman name Aegidius, a 5th century leader, also recorded in a very ancient king-list

---

[*] This *difficult* name is to be preferred to *Frollo,* also found in some manuscripts.

[†] Or, would be if the text were present! The editor makes the perfectly reasonable assumption that the Norman annals were faithfully copied.

as Egegius, of whom more anon, is derived Gilles, in English Giles. The French in the middle ages knew this man as Gillon.*

So, from Flollo → Chlollo, from Chlollo → Chlodio/Chlogio, whom do we discover concealed but the Frankish king? Here we have a realistic opponent of Arthur's, someone who was troublesome enough to have been involved in a serious battle with Aetius C.440. (The Cambrai episode would have been a smaller-scale event.)

What I wish to propose is an unknown battle fought by the Bretons with or without Roman help against the new enemy, in which Arthur had a significant role. We can imagine Geoffrey finding some such sparse entry as: 'Arthur was in the army that fought with Flollo outside Paris and defeated him.' Geoffrey's imagination would do the rest, caring nothing about the Franks, turning Romans into arch-enemies who were competing with Arthur for Europe[5].

Probably fought in the late 440s, this 'battle of Paris', a contest most likely forced by a coalition of Romans and Bretons upon the Frankish enemy, stopped Chlodio and his army yet again as they tried to break away from the Somme towards the Loire.

Worse was still to come for northern Gaul with the arrival of the Huns. This nomadic people had appeared in south-eastern Europe nearly three centuries before. Since 434, they had been ruled by Attila whose brother and co-leader he had murdered in 445. His empire extended from the Alps to the Caspian Sea. He had fought savage campaigns against the Eastern Empire in 441-3 and 447, devastating Greece and the Balkans. Now he turned his attention westward.

---

* Similarly, the Breton King Gradlon sometimes becomes Grallon.

The year was 451 and the great defender of the western empire was waiting for him. Aetius, now about 60, knew Attila and the Huns well, beginning with his days as a hostage. Hunnish mercenaries had been many times employed by him. But latterly the Huns had turned hostile and any alliance with the empire was at an end.

Now, drawing as much as he might on the different groups of Germanic federates resident in Gaul, and above all the powerful Visigoths, he managed to raise a huge army. Following a list provided by the Gothic historian Jordanes in the 6th century, we need not doubt that Armoricans and Bretons were also included.[*]

The great battle that took place soon after, sometimes called the Catalaunian Plain and somewhere near Troyes, was a terrific struggle, leaving what ancient sources reported variously as 162,000 or 300,000 dead. Gibbon has said, 'The nations from the Volga to the Atlantic were assembled.' The Visigothic king, Theodoric, was fatally wounded. But it was the Huns who were compelled to withdraw. They expected pursuit from the army in the field; none came. Both sides had suffered severely. After several days' delay in camp Attila retreated beyond the Rhine: Aetius' coalition had achieved its purpose, though at great cost. Some would add that a great destruction of both Visigoths and Huns was in accord with Roman policy, and that Aetius had no intention of achieving a great Visigothic victory at Hunnish expense.[†]

---

[*] I follow Fleuriot in reading, additionally to the Armoritiani (Armoricans), the Litavii (Bretons) in place of the unknown Litiani.

[†] This battle, often called that of Chalons-sur-Marne in modern times, is differently presented by Professor Kim who sees it as a Hunnish victory and the battle misdescribed on the model of the ancient battle of Marathon.

It is legitimate to ask: could Arthur have been present? To which we can only answer: yes, it is very likely if he was in Brittany. This was a battle for the western empire nor was he the kind of man to shirk a challenge. But there is no evidence of any kind. Our imagination must move us as it chooses.

Chapter 9 - The Continent 452 - 465

The following year Attila turned his attention towards Italy. The passes over the Julian Alps had always been difficult to defend, and Aetius made no effort on Italy's behalf until a force of auxiliaries arrived, with which he made some inroads upon the army of Attila. No one knows if Aetius deliberately abandoned Italy to protect Gaul. A suggestion of his to the emperor Valentinian that Valentinian should make his escape with him was not well received in Italy. However, Attila's invasion was short-lived. He responded to the desperate pleas of an embassy, retired and died shortly after.

A Germanic confederation proceeded to destroy the power of the Huns in 454, and the friendliness of the Visigoths towards Rome spelt further misfortune for Aetius. In no time Valentinian had murdered his great general by his own hand, and six months later, in the spring of 455, he himself was murdered by Huns loyal to Aetius. For Aetius, it was a very sad end to a glittering career, and a dangerous situation for the Western empire.

In Gaul there was a power vacuum, and a man named Aegidius of whose career we have almost no prior knowledge was appointed overall commander, 'magister militum per Gallias' by the emperor Majorian in 457, though he may have borne that title already.

An unusual thing had happened the previous year. The Franks who were having an unhappy time with their new king Childeric, a notorious womanizer,[*] invited Aegidius to be their ruler and he accepted the role.

---

[*] I think this is much more likely than the suggestion that they were rejecting polygamous practice.

Childeric went off into exile in the neighbouring kingdom of Thuringia. Probably he took some loyalists with him, but a substantial portion of the Frankish people was now under Roman control. His contemporary, bishop Hydatius describes Aegidius as 'a man, according to the commendation of rumour, pleasing to God by good works' to which we might add Priscus' statement that, in the 462-3 war against the Goths, Aegidius performed 'the noblest actions of a courageous man'.

Now, if we search for Arthur in the complex web of Continental politics and warfare, we find some extremely surprising mediaeval texts.[*] A learned Franciscan historian, in the latter half of the 14th century, Jacques de Guise, wrote a history of a region of what is now Belgium. He says at one point that this region was oppressed in the time of 'Arthur and the Goths, Huns and Vandals.' And in another place, he declares that Arthur was king during the rule of General Aegidius; which perhaps refers not to the beginning of Aegidius' rule over the Franks but to his period as leader of an independent state, slightly later.

A third reference appears in a 1525 chronicle by Philippe de Vigneulles who mentions Childeric's flight into Thuringia and continues: 'In his place was chosen Gillon the Roman, who was then established at Soissons. And this Gillon, they say, had many dealings with king Arthur of England...'

The first of these three references proposes an Arthur active before Attila's death. And both the other two appear to connect him with Aegidius, whose mediaeval appellation was Gillon - the last text also indicating that Soissons (the capital of his state) had been occupied by

---

[*] These were found in a survey organised by GeoffreyAshe.

Aegidius since 456 or earlier.*

Late as these references are, they stand separate from the rest of the Arthurian tradition. No one else associated Arthur with Goths, Huns, Vandals or Aegidius. Here is a definite linkage of Arthur with known continental events. Dare we ignore it?

What I wish to suggest is that by 450 Arthur had already become a power in Brittany - probably the head of what amounted to a private army - and that by about 456 or shortly after he was working in concert with Aegidius to cope with brigands or Bacaudae or federates who had fallen out of line. A general is not a king, and in calling him king the two writers are probably being influenced by Geoffrey and the whole mediaeval romantic tradition. But here he is where we would expect to find him - a young but seasoned warrior who has an important and decent friend.

Aegidius served under the emperor Majorian. Gibbon sings the praises of this hard-working emperor whose laws were enacted with care and good sense.

But Majorian incurred the enmity of the barbarian emperor-maker of the time, Ricimer, who thought that he had overreached himself. In August 461, on his way home to Rome after a war with the Vandals, having dismissed his allies, Majorian was seized by Ricimer, who stripped him of his robe and diadem and beheaded him after a

---

* Obviously one is free to consider that there has been a confusion between Arthur and Ambrosius. There might also be a confusion between Aegidius and Aetius. But let us take the tradition as it is recorded. One would have expected an association of some kind between Aegidius and Ambrosius, both independently recorded as virtuous men: it is always easy to underestimate the importance of Ambrosius whom no surviving contemporary source mentions.

beating. In his place Ricimer chose the obscure Libius Severus.

Aegidius was furious. He had campaigned with Majorian and was devoted to him. He refused to recognize Severus, and from his independent state based on Soissons, with Frankish support, he attempted to control the Visigoths.

If there is any truth in the stories that he and Arthur had 'many dealings', we should particularly look for them in this period of Aegidius' independent rule when non-Roman friends would be more significant. Unfortunately detail is mostly lacking. But he did have a serious border dispute with the Visigoths in 462-3.

And in the latter year, we read that 'Fretiricus, brother of king Theodoric, launching an uprising against Aegidius… in the Armorican province, with the circle around him, was defeated and killed'.* Such a contest may well have involved a co-ordinated attack between Aegidius and Arthur.

Aegidius died in 464, 'some say by a trap, others poison,'† to be replaced by his son Syagrius. Sadly we know nothing of Syagrius except at the end of his life. No text links him with Arthur.

Returning now to Geoffrey, we arrive at the great setpiece of his book, Arthur's triumphant return to Paris nine years after his defeat of 'Flollo'. Within a short time a deputation arrives from Lucius Hiberius, 'Procurator of the Republic'. Lucius expresses astonishment at the insolence of Arthur who has conquered so much Roman

---

* Near Orléans, according to Marius d'Avenches. The text is from Hydatius. Gregory of Tours indicates Childeric was also on Aegidius' side.

† Gregory of Tours perhaps favours his dying in a plague then current.

territory. Now Arthur must appear in Rome to face charges - or Lucius will invade Arthur's lands. The stage is now set for a confrontation between the two great powers of the western world.

In a skirmish at Autun he takes a beating. Then, marching on to Langres, he makes preparations for another battle. He takes his troops to the 'vallis Siesia' and there has a resounding victory in which Lucius is killed - and his body afterwards sent to Rome as Britain's only tribute.

The great battle, and indeed the whole stage, has little to do with history, though it is odd that Geoffrey picked a site of such obscurity. It has been identified with a place called Saussy, and the very obscurity might suggest there was some battle fought there.

However, all I wish to suggest is that the period from 461 onwards would be an ideal context for Arthur to be in a battle with the Roman authorities. His friend and companion-in-arms Aegidius seething over the murder of Majorian would have dearly loved vengeance upon Ricimer and his puppet-emperor Severus. Aegidius was now independent of Roman control, and he may have discussed with Arthur his desire for revenge: Arthur and Aegidius in a joint action against Severus' army? Unlikely but not unthinkable, especially if Aegidius felt his 'kingdom' of Soissons at stake.*

---

* It is noteworthy that Malory places the battle with Lucius Hiberius not in vallis Siesia (the Valley of Saussy?) but the Vale of Sessoyne which Eugène Vinaver amongst others has identified as Soissons. Nearby Sissonne in Aisne, recorded as Sessonia in 1107, might also be considered. However neither Soissons nor Sissonne are anywhere close to Geoffrey's route to the battle (via Autun and Langres). Priscus records how disagreement with the Goths in Gaul in 462-3 'deterred him [Aegidius]from war against the Italians.' Ricimer had planted Aegidius'

The whole episode is presumably a fantasy of Geoffrey's but I feel that Libius Severus nearest fits the bill historically for an imperial opponent of Arthur.*

---

enemy Agrippinus in Gaul who collaborated with the Goths.

* Geoffrey Ashe favoured the later emperor Glycerius, also recorded as Lucerius. Another, Olybrius is probably the closest linguistically, also apparently recorded as Olyberius. Lyberius could easily expand to Lucius (H)yberius. He was consul in 464. Of course, if Lucius Hiberius were based on an historical figure, he would not necessarily be Roman. Even Attila would not be unthinkable as the original adversary.

Interlude: Cian, the lost Breton bard

A brief list given in the Historia Brittonum records the names of five poets famous, it would seem, around the 5th and 6th centuries. Of Talhaern Tataguen and Bluchbard we know nothing more; of Taliesin[*] and Aneirin I have spoken elsewhere - we are fortunate in the preservation of a number of their works; but it is time for something to be said concerning the fifth - Cian, called Gueinth Guaut.[†]

Cian was an Armorican Briton perhaps of the 5th century.[‡] The early date might help to account for his virulently anti-Christian stance - before Christianity had attained its keenest hold on the populace.

Our knowledge of the bard derives from the popular oral tradition and from the existence of a collection of his Prophecies which were preserved in the Abbey of Landévennec from the 15th century and probably much earlier,[§] where it was consulted by the 18th century scholar Dom. Louis Le Pelletier, who cited some verses from it in his dictionary of 1752.

---

[*] The 11th century Ingomar of St Méen refers to a visit made by Taliesin to Gildas at his abbey of Rhuys in Brittany. It is presumably this reference that Geoffrey picks up on in his Vita Merlini (LL.685-690).

[†] Whose appellation appears to mean something like "wheat of song".

[‡] This is what La Villemarqué believed but the Historia Brittonum says all five poets flourished *at the same time*. If this is true Cian must be dated to the mid or late 6th century. There is an alleged poem of Talhaern's in the Iolo Mss.

[§] The French text is obscure, unfortunately, leaving a doubt what is meant. A middle Breton classic of the 15th century is a dialogue between Arthur and Cian.

Father Gregory of Rostrenen, another 18th century scholar - who had seen the Prophecies in Le Pelletier's hands - tells us they were called (in Breton) Diouganou, that Cian was a "prophet or rather .... astrologer", a native of the *comté* of Goëlo who predicted, "as he himself says, what has happened since in the two Britains." His fame was very great amongst the people at that time, *and such was still the case* when Théodore Hersart de la Villemarqué published his first collection of Breton ballads in 1839. But sadly the manuscript of Cian's Prophecies succumbed to the fury of the French Revolution.

We are thus almost wholly reliant for text upon the fragments preserved from the mouths of the people, though it is pleasing to note that the last line of the main ballad given here corresponds to a line at the beginning of the MS prophecies. "[Cian] notes ..... that he was dwelling between Roc'h-allaz and Porz-Gwenn, in the diocese of Tréguier," says Father Gregory. Like La Villemarqué, Father Gregory prefers to use his popular appellation, Gwenc'hlan.

The first fragment concerns a poor blind old man - surely the poet himself - travelling from district to district on a small white mountain pony, his young son leading it by the bridle. He is searching for a field to cultivate, where also he may build a house. Knowing what plants are grown out of good soil, he asks the boy from time to time, "My son, can you see the clover turning green?" "I only see the foxglove in flower," the boy replies. "Well then, let us go further," responds the old man. And he continues his journey. When he has found the flower he is looking for, he stops. Dismounted and seated on a rock in the sun, he makes clear to his son the best manner to fertilize the soil and the tasks in order required for cultivation in the different seasons. He concludes, "Before the World's end the worst soil will produce the best corn." Mysteriously improbable!*

This tranquil picture is much at variance with his other poetic remains: "The day will come when Christ's priests will be hunted; there will be raised a hue and cry after them as if they were wild beasts." In the ensuing carnage, "they will all die in packs, on Menez-Bré, in legions." At that time (he continues), "the millwheel will grind very small: the blood of the monks will supply its water."

Cian was a fierce hater. Tradition tells us that he was himself pursued by a foreign Christian prince. After being captured by this warrior, Cian had his eyes put out and was thrown into a dungeon where he was left to die. Shortly afterwards, his cruel enemy died on the battlefield fighting with Bretons.

The following ballad, supposed to have been written a few days before Cian's death, was recited to La Villemarqué in Melgven and appears to be at one with the tradition. Though the language must have changed considerably, the meaning and the sentiments may be a very close reflection of Cian's original words. Through this powerful piece of writing, Cian's personality stands forth poignantly in all its rage and hatred, the bitter memories and despair.

When the sun sets, when the sea swells,
    I sing at my threshold.

---

* Found in the collection of Jean-Marie de Penguern. This fragment may be *about* Cian and not by him. As a blind prophet he is likely to be the subject. See Laurent's Aux Sources Du Barzaz-Breiz P.18 for a part of the text.

When I was young I would sing,
> Now I am old, I sing still.

I sing by night, I sing by day, and yet I feel gloom.
If my head is downcast, and I feel gloom, I have reason.
It's not that I am fearful: I have no fear of being put to death.
It's not that I am fearful: I have lived long enough.
When you do not look for me, you will find me.
And when you look for me, you will not find me.[*]
It's a small matter what's going to happen: what must be will be.
All must die thrice before the final repose.

I see the wild boar coming out of the wood; he limps badly; he has been wounded in the foot.
Mouth wide open and filled with blood, mane white with age,
He is surrounded by his young, squealing with hunger.

I see the seahorse come to his rendezvous with him,
Making the seashore shake with terror.
He is white as shining snow; he bears on his forehead horns of silver.
The water bubbles under him, in the fire of the thunder from his nostrils.
Two seahorses accompany him, as close as the grass on the edge of the pond.

Stand firm! stand firm, seahorse!
Strike him on the head, strike hard, and again!
Bare feet glide through blood.
> Harder still! Strike then! Harder still!

---

[*] This and the preceding line may be interpolated.

I see the blood like a torrent.
> Strike then! Strike hard! Harder still!

I see the blood rising to his knee.
> The blood is like a pool!

Harder still! Strike then! Harder still! You can rest tomorrow.
Strike hard! Strike hard, seahorse!
Strike him on the head! Strike hard! Again!

As I slept soundly in my cold tomb,
I heard the eagle calling in
the middle of
the night.
He was calling to his eaglets
> and all the birds
>> of heaven.

This is what he said as
> he called to them:

"Rise up quickly on your
> two wings!

It isn't the rotten flesh of
> dogs or sheep: it's

Christian flesh we must be after!"
"Listen, old sea raven.[*] Tell me,
> what's that you're holding?"

"I am holding the General's head.
> I want his two red eyes.

 I am seizing his two eyes
> because he has seized yours."

"And you, fox, tell me: what is
> it that you are holding?"

---

[*] Corvus marinus = cormorant.

"I hold his heart, which was
    as false as mine;
Which has desired your death
    and for a long time has
        kept you dying."
"And you, toad, tell me: what
    are you doing there at
        the corner of his mouth?"
"I have been set here to
    await his soul on its journey.
 It will reside in me so long
    as I live; in punishment
for the crime he has committed:
Against the Bard who lives no
    longer between Roc'h-allaz and Porz-Gwenn.

It would be tempting, taking one's cue from '*Culhwch and Olwen*', to see in the seahorse and his two associates Arthur, Cei and Bedwyr, and in the boar with his brood, a prototype of Arthur's legendary adversary, Twrch Trwyth.

Chapter 10 - Britain 452 - 467

The Germanic invaders' fortunes appear to have been in the ascendant in Britain for many years after their breakout, following the death of Vortimer. The letter to Aetius is testimony to this, though it uses the word 'barbarians', not (as we might expect) 'Saxons'. (It would be foolish to suppose the Picts and Scots were suddenly inactive, but most likely occupied in other parts of the country than the south-east.)

We may suppose the Britons to have been leaving for the continent in large numbers, and, despite the efforts that the resistance under Ambrosius would have been making, there are no records of any victories - though Wippedsfleot in 444 may have been one.

The Anglo-Saxon Chronicle for the year 452 carries a starkly disturbing entry: 'In this year Hengest and Aesc fought against the Welsh and captured innumerable spoils, and the Welsh fled from the English like fire'.[*]

Gildas may be remembering the same event: '... A fire heaped up and nurtured by the hand of the impious easterners spread from sea to sea. It devastated town and country round about and, once it was alight, it did not die down until it had burned almost the whole surface of the island *and was licking the western ocean with its fierce red tongue.*' I do not think the A-S Chronicle is describing a single battle, but a series of encounters in which the defenders fled before the Kentish men, unable to offer any serious resistance. Gildas' text suggests a drive across southern

---

[*] Earle and Plummer would make this the last battle for the conquest of Kent, but Crayford was so substantial a British defeat that this seems unlikely. And why not name the battle site?

Britain from Kent, finishing probably in Dumnonia. This great western raid, as suggested by Gildas' text, can hardly be much earlier, for it would be strange if the Saxons failed to record it, or much later, when the Saxon threat had clearly diminished. Nor are there later A-S Chronicle entries down to the time of Gildas that might correspond to it. Gildas' text is vague enough to be taken as a general statement about Saxon expansion, but his mention of their reaching the western ocean is a graphic notice of something more specific, of a time when Hengest and Aesc[*] went far outside their south-eastern haunts. No other evidence of this great raid survives now except perhaps for a single indication that must be used with caution, the evidence of place-names.

Across the south-west there is a thin scattering of names that may commemorate Hengest. But 'hengest' is also the Old English word for 'stallion'; (Hengest's alleged brother's name which has come down to us as Horsa, 'horse' or, more probably 'mare', seems to have developed out of this meaning.)

Hengesthill[†] somewhere north of Exeter and named in Risdon's survey of Devon is one. Henceford, formerly He(n)g(e)stforde in the region of Thelbridge; Hence Moor, formerly Hengis(t)more near Honiton; Henscott (Heyng(e)stecote) near Bradford; Hensleigh farm (Heng(e)steleg) near Tiverton; Henstridge wood (Hengestridge); and Hingston Down near Moretonhampstead, formerly Henges(t)don. This list

---

[*] Gildas might however be referring to the northern exploits of Octa: it may be observed, for instance, how Gwalchmei was expelled from Galloway in the west. (See Cap 11).

[†] Unless this is modern Henstill, which has a different derivation.

might be amplified with the Hinkseys of Oxfordshire: Hengestesie(g) perhaps equating to Hengest's Island; Hengistbury Head near Bournemouth on the south coast; and of special interest is Hingston Down near Gunnislake in Cornwall, a battle site in 835 where English names are uncommon. It seems only right to allow the distinct possibility that *some* of these names may relate not to horses but Hengest himself. And Hingston Down might suggest a battle beside the river Tamar, the last main line of Dumnonian defence before the heartland was reached and also of some proximity to Tintagel. (The 835 battle was a drive *eastward* by Danish pirates and Cornish men which was stopped by King Egbert of Wessex.*)

This great raid, a huge English success, brought the British to a new pitch of gloom, and probably triggered more mass migrations to the Continent.† We know of a British bishop on Gallic soil in 461 who clearly had no Gallic see.

But here the Anglo-Saxon Chronicle speaks eloquently to us by its silence: there was no follow-up. Something changed which we do not understand. I believe

---

* The genitive form of Hengest (with 's') is often lacking in these examples, but such might easily be the case with a very ancient placename that was also awkward to pronounce. In my vicinity, we have Hexworthy understood to be Hex*tes* + worthy, but it is no surprise if in old records the 's' form is often missing. These *hengest* names appear exclusive to Southwestern Britain.

† A raid of such daring might seem impossible, but one would have to know the circumstances of the moment. It is said that with equal daring the Comanche Indians of North America used to raid the fringes of the Aztec Empire far to the south. For those who demur, I might point out that Arthur's greatest battle has often been placed at Bath, in the far west. And this was apparently at a time of British success!

that this raid was effectively responsible for a series of British victories beginning C.453 though we have no record of them.

It would be tempting to place Arthur's return to Britain about this time - I would actually suspect he regularly crossed the channel between Gaul and Britain in adulthood. Another significant factor, as well as his visits to relatives, might well be Ogyrfan ruler of Cabeiliauc,[*] a little province that roughly corresponded to the old Montgomeryshire in mid-Wales. Perhaps Arthur had known him from his childhood by Bala Lake. Ogyrfan might even have been the son of King Anblaud, Arthur's grandfather, and therefore Arthur's own uncle. The romances have Arthur helping Ogyrfan against powerful British enemies. But at any rate Arthur fell in love with and married Ogyrfan's daughter probably about now. Her name was Gwenhwyfar - Guinevere.

One would guess that Ambrosius' leadership lay behind the successes of this period. Different endings are given to Vortigern's life, none of them good. Perhaps the most likely is: 'When he was hated for his sin ... by all men of his own nation ... he wandered from place to place until at last his heart broke, and he died without honour.' Lewis Thorpe, the Penguin translator of Geoffrey, noted in 1964 that there had recently been three old ladies named Vertigen in Wallingford, Oxfordshire running a sweetshop who claimed descent from Vortigern. The name Wallingford implies an enclave of Britons in Saxon territory, and this is where he and his entourage

---

[*] Leodegrance of Cameliard, in the romances. 'Leod' appears to be a title, but perhaps truncated. There is no difficulty in 'egrance' being derived from Ogyrfan, perhaps through a Latin form such as Oguranus; likewise, Cameliard from Cabeiliauc.

may finally have settled. Only in Brittany was he remembered kindly, being oddly enough revered as a saint.[*]

The Historia Brittonum tells us that Vortigern's third son, Pascent, 'ruled in the two countries called Builth and Gwerthrynion after his father's death, by permission of Ambrosius, who was ... king among all the kings of the British nation.' This is a clear indication of a new paramount sovereign. But precisely what Ambrosius achieved in this period we do not know. The great earthwork, the Wansdyke,[†] between Bath and Salisbury, seems to belong to it though in two pieces not necessarily of the same date. The magnanimity to the son of his enemy suggests a unified Britain under a good leader, whom Gildas praises.

The excellent 12th century historian William of Malmesbury tells us:

'Ambrosius ... quelled the presumptuous barbarians by the powerful aid of warlike Arthur.' This is a reasonable deduction, but one may doubt whether it was founded on any particular evidence. What William would have certainly believed was that Arthur completed what Ambrosius started - the rout of the opposition. William is implying a connexion between these two men that he

---

[*] There is a record of his mortal remains being kept at Quimperlé, but this may be someone else of the same name. In the late 18th century a stone coffin containing the skeleton of a tall man was discovered at Bedd Gwrtheyrn i.e. Vortigern's grave, near Llithfaen in N. Wales.

[†] The name is derived from the Saxon god Woden and seems to indicate that the Saxons who named it were ignorant of its origins. Another earthwork, part of Offa's Dyke in Welsh border country near Chirk, has lately been found to be possibly as early as the 5th century.

could not prove. But I have little doubt that he is right.

The shadowy figure of Ambrosius has his own links with the Continent. A very ancient Irish version of the Historia Brittonum calls Ambrosius 'king of the Franks and the Armorican Britons'. This is early in his career when Vortigern feels threatened by him. It is hard to know what to make of this, but his faction may have been based in Brittany in the 420s and early 430s. He could have been king of one of the regions with some Franks under his jurisdiction.[*] But on the whole it is easier to see him acquiring power in Brittany in the 450s and 460s on the back of his British success.[†]

Léon Fleuriot has drawn attention to the one-time existence of an earthwork north-east of Vannes in Southern Brittany. The parish now called Mangolerian was called in the 9th century Ran Macoer Aurilian, 'a piece of the wall of Aurelian'; and at Le Château in Larré, twenty kilometres eastward, a second Macoer Aurilian was also standing.

Though Aurelian may be the third century emperor (who did spend some time in Gaul and is renowned for his work on the walls of Rome) or any other person of that name, it is very plausible that our Ambrosius Aurelianus had this wall built or begun, probably to defend Vannes, an important Gallo-Roman city and also perhaps his Breton headquarters, from southern and eastern invaders. It is possible to identify him with Allanius[‡] named as a (Gallic) Roman 'king' in an ancient

---

[*] As Gradlon is also said to have been (Landévennec Cartulary).

[†] The remote hilltop site in Wales, Dinas Emrys, suggests itself as his headquarters in the early days of the fighting i.e. 436-452.

[‡] But apparently pre-dating Aetius. A king of Vannes, Eusebius is recorded

king-list that includes Aetius and Aegidius. Many names are distorted; Allanius might derive from Alianus, a straightforward abridgement of Aurelianus' name. The later Breton saint, Paulus Aurelianus, was probably of his family.

At some time in the 450s, it is reasonable to believe that Arthur, after his marriage in Britain to a Welsh princess or chieftain's daughter, and Ambrosius, the enterprising British leader of great experience, would have met and conversed - the two army chiefs with a common interest at heart, the protection of the British, at home or abroad. Perhaps Ambrosius requested Arthur's help, but the 'dealings' with Aegidius would seem to anchor Arthur firmly on the Continent for some years.[*] It is probably the subsequent decade, and perhaps after Aegidius' death that Arthur chose to return permanently to the land of his birth. The Historia Brittonum gives us a starting-point of 467 for his British victories, following the death of Hengest.

---

ruling in the early 6th century. Caradawc Vreichvras is also tenuously associated with Vannes.

[*] It remains possible that their 'dealings' primarily concerned naval patrols in the Channel, but there is no tradition of Arthur as a seaman.

Chapter 11 - Arthur in Britain - The Battle-list

Sometime in the 460s, perhaps following the murder of his friend Aegidius and about the time his illustrious cousin Illtud reverted from military life to the monastic, Arthur made his permanent home in Britain. It is easy to believe that this was at the request of Ambrosius, who had perhaps witnessed Arthur's activities at close quarters in Brittany.

We must now consider the Historia Brittonum's battle-list datable to this part of Arthur's life. Hengest had died, and his son or grandson, had come down from the north, where he had been based for some time, to take the military leadership in Kent.

William of Malmesbury adds the interesting detail that Hengest's brother and nephew or grandson (which we perhaps can correct, from the Historia Brittonum, to Hengest's son and his cousin Ebissa) had expelled Arthur's nephew, Walwen (Gwalchmei) from his northern kingdom named as Galloway, in modern-day south-west Scotland. But the similarity of the Latin names for Gwalchmei and Galloway may give us pause for thought. It is said that Arthur's sister married a northern ruler. And there is an odd early 12th century text identified recently from the writings of Lambert of St Omer; in which we are led to believe that there was a palace in the land of the Picts belonging to Arthur 'the soldier' in which sculptures of all the main events of his life were to be found. Did his sister's dynasty survive the expulsion of Gwalchmei? Or was Gwalchmei reinstated by Arthur?[6]

The battle-list is generally considered to be a translation (into Latin) of a poem in Brythonic or Welsh.

If Arthur had a court bard, the original might even have been his work. Scholars have translated several of the Latin expressions back to the initial text. The word 'shoulders' in the original would be remarkably similar to that for 'shield', and the confident surmise is that the translator was in error. The text is preceded by a preamble:

'At that time the Saxons increased in number and grew in Britain. Following the death of Hengist, his son Octha crossed from north Britain to the kingdom of the Kentishmen, and from him arose their kings.[*] Then Arthur was fighting against them in those days alongside the kings of the Britons, but he himself, was commander-in-chief [literally, 'leader in the fighting']:[†]

The 1st battle was at the mouth of the river called Glein.

The 2nd, 3rd, 4th, and 5th on another river called Dubglas in the region of Linnuis.

The 6th battle on a river called Bassas.

The 7th battle was in Celidon wood i.e Cat Coit Celidon.

The 8th battle was in Castle Guinnion, in which Arthur carried an image of the holy Mary, everlasting

---

[*] There is some confusion. The royal family of Kent took their name from Aesc: the Aescingas. I suggest Octa is Aesc's son, and he came down from the north at the behest of his father.

[†] The Latin term corresponding to 'Leader in the fighting' is *dux bellorum*. This looks like a straightforward translation of the Brythonic *Catigern*. So this may have been a title Arthur was known by in his own day - pretty much the equivalent of *amheraudur* (derived from the Roman *imperator* and best translated as 'general' or 'commander - in - chief'). Because of the confusion between names and titles, Vortimer's brother Catigern may be a phantom, and in reality a description of Vortimer himself, though the genealogies give Catigern a descendant.

virgin on his shoulders; and the pagans were turned to flight on that day and there was a great slaughter of them through the power of our Lord Jesus Christ and of holy Mary his virgin mother.

The 9th battle was fought in the City of the Legion.

The 10th battle was fought on the bank of the river called Tribruit.

The 11th battle was on a mountain called Agned.

The 12th battle was on the mountain of Badon in which fell in one day 960 men by one attack of Arthur's, and no one laid them low but himself alone. And in every battle he proved victorious.'

The compiler concludes by telling us how the defeated Saxons sought help from Germany and more and more arrived down to the time of Ida, a king of Northumbria in the mid-sixth century - a period of some 80 years.

It is apposite to make some remarks upon this list, the subject of discussion over centuries. The battles are said to have occurred at a time when Saxon numbers were growing - perhaps the consequence of an initial summons from Hengest for help from Germany, though the British settlement would also bring a new generation into the picture.

The Historia Brittonum sees Arthur as a warrior leader but not a king, fighting against the Kentishmen (and others?) led by Hengest's son after Hengest's death, who are fighting from Kent.

The river Glein, scene of the first battle, may be the river Glen in Lincolnshire or Northumbria. The area to the north of the Lincolnshire Glen was settled early, and the river is much farther south than the other. But the Northumbria site is close to a huge Iron Age hill fort which was reoccupied in the post-Roman period:

Yeavering Bell provided such an important defensive position that it subsequently became the site of King Edwin of Northumbria's palace.

This river Glen, curving round the southern edge of the former Wooler Park, falls into the Till a little eastward. Two ancient swords were discovered in the Park in 1814 standing perpendicularly as if thrust down for concealment. A Saxon fibula has also been found in the south-east corner of Millfield Plain (where the great battle of Flodden was fought in 1513) close by, on a bank of the river. Here also Paulinus carried out mass baptisms in the early 7th century, in the waters of the *Gleni*. The British seem to have maintained that these baptisms including King Edwin's were at the hands of Run Map Urbagen, (who contributed to the Historia Brittonum).

The next four battles are thought to be one only, spread over four verses of the supposed original poem. Douglas is a desperately common name, and 'Linnuis' is unidentified though perhaps derived from Lindum (Lincoln) and possibly placing the battle in Lincolnshire. An old gloss on Ranulph Higden's chronicle places the Douglas near Wigan in Lancashire where it is still to be found. Bassas is no less difficult. Baschurch in Shropshire is one suggestion, for those who believe that the nearby river Perry was Bassas previously. (But rivers are notorious for hanging on to their ancient names).

Celidon Wood is generally believed to be the ancient Caledonian Wood of southern Scotland, but this is a very large area.

Castle Guinnion is very similar to the old name for the Roman fort of Binchester near Durham. The Greek and Latin names might easily suggest a Celtic form Guinnuion that the compiler misread or miscopied. The City of the Legion is likely to be Chester - formerly known as Carlegion - or Caerleon, still preserving 'legion' in altered form. While Caerleon fell on quiet days latterly in the Roman period, Chester was refortified in the 4th century. Its legion, the XX Valeria Victrix, was the last stationed in Britain, so Chester must be favoured.

The Tribruit is unknown. A very early Welsh poem tells us that 'they fell by hundreds before Bedwyr... on the strands of Tryfrwyd fighting with Garwlwyd.' The context seems to be a northern one. Gwrgi Garwlwyd is mentioned in the Triads as an oppressor of the Cymry (British) and apparently from the North.

Mount Agned carries the important early gloss: (Cat) *Breguoin*, thought to equate with Bremenium, the Roman fort at High Rochester in the north. Now Geoffrey of Monmouth, who cherrypicks from the battle-list to give Arthur a few choice victories and omits others on the list altogether, has no Agned. But he does include a Mount Damen, where a battle is won by Uther Pendragon. In the Welsh version of the history in Jesus College, Oxford, this mountain is called Mynydd danned (the toothed mountain). Could the compiler of the Historia Brittonum have read something like this in an original battle-list? Could he have transposed a 'd', thus mistakenly altering 'dagned' to 'agned' or misreading or miswriting 'danned'?[7]

A Welsh monk, Madoc compiling his own version of Geoffrey's History around 1300, tells us that Mount Damen is above the head of Chochem - possibly Windy Crag or Windy Gyle at the headwaters of the river Coquet. These are to be found north-west of High Rochester. Wingates, despite its commanding view that includes the eastern seaboard, is less likely, being fifteen miles east of High Rochester and nowhere near the headwaters. We therefore have a possible site for Mount Agned in close proximity to a site for Breguoin. There is a 6th century poem of Taliesin's referring to fighting in the 'cells of Brewyn'; this is not Arthurian but may indicate the significance of the area.[*]

So we are little the wiser near the end of the list. Southern Scotland ... Chester... possibly Binchester and, most convincingly, near High Rochester. There is a northern *feeling* as if this was the main theatre of operations, and one is bound to consider opposition to the budding north-eastern Saxon kingdoms of Deira and Bernicia. Brave people have attempted to link these battles in a continuous campaign, but there is no evidence for this. It is however difficult to believe that these victories were all achieved against the same enemy, though it is odd that we cannot relate any of them to the environs of Kent.[†8]

---

[*] Taliesin's battle, won by Urien of Rheged in the mid or late 6th century, is called 'the battle of the cells of Brewyn long celebrated'. Thus it appears to take place in the fort, not at the nearby mountain. (The fort was probably occupied by the Saxons.) I cannot favour any argument equating the two battles.

[†] The following early glosses or variants may be of interest, as recorded in Giles' old translation: '... though there were many noble than himself, yet he was twelve times chosen their commander'; '... the City of Legion which is called Cair Lion.' '... a most severe contest, when Arthur penetrated to the hill of Badon.' The writer of the first text certainly does not see Arthur as a king.

Chapter 12 - Déols and Riothamus

Before we look at the final battle on the list, let us consider Arthur's position. Aged about forty, he has arrived in Britain, perhaps at Ambrosius' personal request, after a successful career in Brittany. He has linked with chieftains across Britain and fought beside them as their military commander. He has achieved breathtaking success, though this is not to pretend there might not have been other battles quietly forgotten.

But, in the midst of this, is it possible to believe that he travelled abroad again to fight one of the most significant battles of his life? This is no absurd suggestion, for the circumstances were highly unusual.

Let us set the scene with the words of Jordanes: 'Euric, king of the Visigoths, aware of the frequent change of Roman emperors, endeavoured to take Gaul in his own right'.

The year is probably 469. The then emperor, Anthemius, was in a tricky position. Promoted to the throne in 467, he was not on easy terms with the man who had enthroned him - the barbarian, Ricimer, Majorian's murderer (who as a barbarian could not himself be emperor). Marrying Anthemius' daughter did not bind them as close as it might. One stood for the conservative aristocracy of Italy and old imperial values; the other was part of the new order, linked by blood with the Sueves on his father's side, with the Visigoths on his mother's - she was a king's daughter - and with the Burgundians by marriage, being brother-in-law to their king, Gundioc.

Anthemius wished to weaken Ricimer's barbarian support, and to that end tried to instil stronger imperial sentiments in Gaul and Spain. Amongst other efforts, Anthemius' predicament led to a very surprising choice: he sought help from Britain* against the Visigoths. Still more surprisingly, the Britons came. It appears, from a long blockade of Paris believed to have been instigated by the Franks in 465, that the Franks, having broken with Syagrius as well as the central Roman government, had been driven back to the Somme in the north-east, ceasing temporarily to be a dominant power in Gaul. Fleuriot would date Ambrosius' title, 'King of the Franks', from this time. For some Frankish settlers would not have retreated with Childeric but accepted a new overlord.

So British ships carrying an army of supposedly 12,000 men sailed to the mouth of the Loire on the north-west coast, perhaps replenishing their provisions at Vannes. But Nantes, another Gallo-Roman city a short distance up the Loire, was an even more opportune destination. They sailed as far as Bourges and disembarked, occupying the town. Their leader is given as Riothamus (Riotimus). He is 'king of the Britons', and quite probably paramount sovereign like Ambrosius.†

It is now that a remarkable letter from Arvandus, Praetorian Prefect in Gaul, was intercepted on its way to Euric, the king of the Visigoths. Friendly with the Visigoths and in the pocket of Ricimer, Arvandus proposed to Euric that he abandon his peaceful stance

---

* If they were in fact Bretons, it is hard to see the necessity of a sea-journey. But possibly this is a Breton force supplemented by new British arrivals. Some find in this expedition evidence for a great British migration, but there seems nothing peaceful in its intentions.

† Riothamus must not be confused with another leader Iaun Reith who crossed to Brittany perhaps at the beginning of the 6th century with many followers.

Déols and Riothamus | 63

toward Anthemius, attack the British force,* and carve Gaul up between Goths and Burgundians. Sent to Rome on a charge of treason, Arvandus narrowly escaped the death penalty.

Within a very short time 'Euric … came against them and, [having driven them from the town], after a long fight, he routed Riotimus … before the Romans could join him'.† The survivors fled with their king to the Burgundians. This made for an interesting situation. The Burgundian king Gundioc - it does not seem that his successor was yet upon the throne - was as we have seen a brother-in-law, and a close supporter, of Ricimer's. To help Anthemius' allies was to risk Ricimer's wrath, especially considering they had come to Gaul to fight his friends the Visigoths. But the Burgundians were Roman federates and loyalists, and, to avoid giving massive offence to their emperor, they acceded to Riothamus' request for asylum while no doubt encouraging him to leave as soon as decently possible. In any case we can have some confidence that the result of the battle was much to Ricimer's liking, and he was perhaps capable of magnanimity in the circumstances. It is certainly hard to believe that Gundioc did not consult Ricimer on this sensitive issue.

---

* 'The Britons beyond the Loire' appear to be Riothamus' army. The casual description suggests this was not Arvandus' 1st letter; 'beyond' means south of the Loire, not north as usually stated. I owe this information to Stephen Terry.

† The battle site was Bourg-de-Déols near Châteauroux, beside the river Indre.

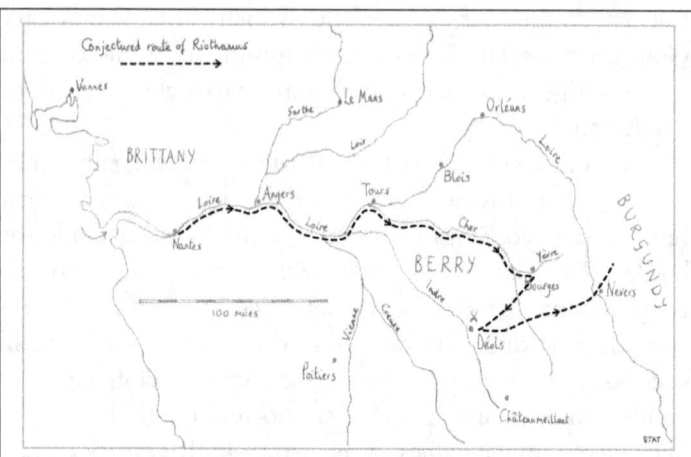

It is not possible to be confident about Riothamus' movements. Arvandus' 'Britons beyond the Loire' ought to be north of the Loire, for he addresses a king based to the south in Toulouse, but they must be south, according to our available knowledge. Sidonius' letter suggests an encampment, not quartering within Bourges, but he describes the mood of the soldiers in very positive terms – unlikely after a major defeat.

And why does Riothamus head towards Brittany? For escape from an overwhelming force? Or for a rendezvous with the Romans? But which? Syagrius' men or Anthemius' men or simply Romans out of Brittany?

And why change direction after the battle, travelling east to Burgundy? Burgundy was loyal to the empire, but Brittany should also have been a safe destination. There may be a hidden aspect in all this: Euric's skilful military manoeuvring.

Riothamus fades from history at this point but for a single letter written to him by bishop Sidonius Apollinaris, a literary Gallo-Roman who had led a deputation to Anthemius in 467. The letter is thought to have been sent after the defeat. Its purpose is to persuade Riothamus to return some slaves who have been enticed from their owner by certain of Riothamus' followers. Sidonius paints a picture of the solitary complainant going in amongst 'worldly, raucous armed men made over-confident by courage, by numbers and camaraderie'; so if this is really after the battle, it must be some little while. (I would place this letter *before* the battle, for, though many survived the battle, there is no indication here of the demoralization that naturally follows a significant defeat.)

But in one passage the writer talks of Riothamus directly: 'I myself bear witness to the burden of your sensitivity, which invariably finds expression in that delicacy that you should blush for others' faults.' This is the single personal detail and strangely reminiscent of Gildas' description of Ambrosius - 'a modest[*] man'. We see the likelihood that Riothamus was well-known for actual blushing. I suggest that Ambrosius was also.

An argument based on blushing is not of the strongest kind. But why should Ambrosius and Riothamus not be one and the same? Riothamus may be a title - it is Brythonic for 'kingliest' - just such as we might expect a Roman leader of Britons to assume or be given.[†]

---

[*] In Latin, 'modestus' (modest) and 'verecundus' from verecundia (delicacy) are practically interchangeable. One might think Riothamus was well-known to the bishop and probably had territory under his rule in Britain and Brittany.

[†] Iaun Reith whose second name is assumed as a Breton form of the Latin manuscript original, also had a son who may have been a blusher - Daniel Dremrud i.e. Redface. Daniel appears by a distortion of his nickname to have been turned into 'Budicius', whose representation is said to be found in Quimper Cathedral (See Fleuriot P.190). An identification between Iaun Reith and Riothamus is improbable. Iaun Reith is presumably Iona *son of Riatam* named in the St Brieuc Chronicle as of a royal lineage. (He is probably also Iona King of France in *Culhwch and Olwen*). This would rule out the identification of Riothamus with Ambrosius (for the lineage is from Riwal the Marvellous, probably a Briton) unless we accept the lineage as in

I see the battle as one of the last acts in the life of Ambrosius, responding to the call of the western emperor.* Evidently there was a plan to link with a Roman force (under Syagrius?), but Euric was too quick, and an opportunity was lost, though events were to prove the greatest threat was from another quarter.

The last question to ask is: if this battle was fought by a British king with a huge army - and it must have been very large to take on a nation - whether or not that king was Ambrosius, was Arthur the commander?

Ambrosius himself if indeed present was obviously a superior military leader, and to leave Arthur behind in Britain would normally have made sense. But here was a special moment affecting potentially the whole western Roman empire, for Gaul had long been the crucible in which the fates of nations were decided. It is surely feasible to suggest that Ambrosius or any other leader of this large army might have had his forces taking orders from the new younger military leader with experience of the terrain. But again we have no evidence in favour of this. Nor can we tell what the situation was at that moment at home in Britain, though the expedition suggests Britain was in good heart.

---

the female line. No surviving genealogy includes Ambrosius (Emrys) despite his having many descendants.

* The unlikely event of a British force on the continent becomes more likely if a *Roman* leader in Britain is responding to the emperor.

Chapter 13 - Mount Badon

There are three early mentions of the battle of Mount Badon, the last battle of the Historia Brittonum's list, in the texts that have come down to us. In the battle-list we have seen that Arthur alone laid them low, and in one single attack he killed 960 of the enemy - a not very believable total.

In the 10th century Annales Cambriae we read under a year reckoned to be according to the annalist 516: 'the battle of Badon in which Arthur carried the cross of our Lord Jesus Christ three days and nights on his shoulders [reckoned to be the annalist's error for 'shield'] and the Britons were victors.'

And from Gildas we learn the following: that under Ambrosius' leadership (whose own parents had been killed in the disturbances) the Britons took up arms and won a battle; and from that time victory went either way 'until the year of the siege of Mount Badon, almost the last and one of the greatest slaughters of the wretches, and which was the beginning of the 44th year (as I am well aware), one month already over; which is also my birth-year.'

Putting these sources together, we see that the battle was a siege lasting three or four days, in which Arthur carried a shield with a cross painted on it - surely with the emperor Constantine in mind.[*] Arthur had a main part in this battle to the point of exclusivity: this seems to indicate that only his own troops took part without recourse to the armies of other leaders.

The alarmingly large figure of 960 enemy killed in one

---

[*] Before the battle of the Milvian Bridge, he was told in a dream to place crosses on his soldiers' shields.

assault can perhaps be made more credible as follows: 3 was a special number for the ancient British as witnessed by their Triads - pieces of information grouped in threes. If the original writer had told how Arthur had killed three times twenty and three times three, we have a total: 69. But if the writer continued 'men of Kent', then the next word might be 'Cant' - for instance, Kent was called Cantia by the compiler. So we could have 3 x 20 and 3 x 3 'cant' [men] misunderstood as 60 and 900, if 'Cant' [Kent] were mistaken for 'cant' [a hundred]. This revised text would also name the enemy as Saxons from the south-east, as we would expect.*

The meaning of Gildas' text has been much disputed, but it is clear to me as it was to Bede that the 44 years period is to be understood from a starting- point, one named by Gildas as the beginning of the war under Ambrosius, and by Bede as the Saxons' arrival into Britain, until the war's conclusion at Badon. Gildas may have been told of this timespan by his own family, and dating from Ambrosius' campaigning seemed reasonable to him, though he may have been unaware of Vortimer's efforts previously.

He would be quite certain of the year of Badon even down to the month, for he was born in the same year and must have been told: 'You were three months old when Badon took place' or 'you were born the month after Badon'. Gildas dates the battle to the second month of the year, February.

---

* Probably the compilers of the Historia Brittonum were aware of Kent as a meaning, but I am suggesting that Nennius, the last, made a mistake. (The British form of the name is given as *Chent* in Cap. 37, but perhaps the compiler found a form in an old source that he failed to recognize, especially in view of the neat maths.)

This is a winter siege and, one would suppose, following a daring surprise attack. Convention has proposed the Saxons attacked the Britons. But sieges when they fail are normally called off with the departure of the besieging force. Surely it was the bold general Arthur who launched the siege, surrounding an encampment of the Kentish men perhaps in their own territory. Liddington Castle at Badbury in Wiltshire, has been suggested as a site. This is in what might have been a no man's land east of Dumnonia, a huge earthwork just above the ancient track known as the Ridgeway, and standing nearly a thousand feet high, an excellent vantage point for its environs[9].

In line with the compiler of the Historia Brittonum, we should look for a date in the reign of Hengest's successor (467-491), and taking our starting-point for the 44-year period from Ambrosius' break with Vitalinus (436), we may be correct in placing the siege in 479: this would give Gildas 91 years of life, long but not impossibly long.[*]

The siege of Mount Badon was the crowning achievement of Arthur's life and the start of a long period of peace[10]. Constantius, the biographer of Germanus, writing about 480, calls Britain 'most opulent', imparting a sense of prosperity and harmony.

Ambrosius was surely dead by now, perhaps having only briefly survived the battle of Déols. His dynasty persisted, and his grandson, Aurelius Cynon is castigated by Gildas for 'parricides, fornications, adulteries', and looting and warfare amongst his own people[11]. Gildas ascribes to a man who may be Cynon's son (Cynlas) some

---

[*] Genevieve and Illtud are further examples of aged saints in this period, Genevieve quite probably over 90.

exclusive weaponry perhaps derived from Ambrosius' war manuals.

It would be pleasing to identify Ambrosius as the author of the following text quoted by Gildas:[*] 'We keenly desire that the enemies of the church be our enemies also without any treaty, and that its friends and defenders be accounted not only our federates but also our fathers and lords.'[12] This message of tolerance and friendship towards those friendly to the church is the kind of olive branch that such a king might have held out to newcomers willing to fit into the existing culture and not overtly give offence or resort to violence. Clearly spoken by a secular figure,[†] the passage comes out of the thought of a progressive and educated man willing to accommodate on certain conditions those foreigners who might automatically be viewed by many as enemies. He falls a long way short of demanding pagan conversion to Christianity[13].

---

[*] 92.3 Almost the only quotation in Gildas not identified. For some reason the quotation *quis victurus est* at 62.3 has not been recognized as from Numbers 24.23.

[†] Treating as his own enemies [i.e. on the battlefield] the enemies of the church and refusing to enter into treaties with them. The whole passage reads as a statement of intent but expressed as one of inclination. It may have been taken out of a public proclamation. Gildas had pitifully few late literary sources of a non-Christian kind. Could this text not have come from the same collection in which he found the Letter to Aetius? Even the usurper Constantine was apparently unknown to Gildas. As Gildas himself says, too many documents had crossed the sea - surely to Brittany.

Devastation by the Saxons and others. Or were abandoned and burned out Roman settlements misunderstood by Gildas?

The Massacre of the Concilium. A Tudor representation of the Saxons' gross act of treachery against Vortigern's unarmed council.

FIG. 1.—*Tintagel Castle as represented by Norden, 1584–1600.*

Tintagel, alleged birthplace of Arthur.

King Gradlon of Cornouaille, as represented on Quimper cathedral. Quimper, where Arthur and Leonora fell in love, was his capital.

Honorius. Emperor at the time of the sack of Rome (410), his reign witnessed the end of Roman rule in Britain.

Valentinian III. Supported by the great Aetius, he ruled the Empire for 30 years till his murder in 455 (following his own mad killing of Aetius).

Petronius Maximus. His brief usurpation after Valentinian ended in his murder. He appears to have been a cousin of Pascent, Vortigern's son.

Majorian. This decent emperor's execution by Ricimer in 461 led to his loyal supporter Aegidius' independent rule at Soissons.

Libius Severus, Ricimer's puppet-emperor (461 - 5), possibly an original for Geoffrey's Lucius Hiberius, Arthur's great legendary opponent.

Anthemius, emperor in 469 when he requested Riothamus' help against the Goths.

> inta- de furciferis non minimæ stragis; quique quadragesimus quartus (ut novi)
> ur. annus, mense jam uno emenso, qui & meæ nativitatis est : &, qui illi,
> fuisse dicitur, Britannicorum Bardorum princeps Thaliessinus:
>
> > Gwae yntwy yr ynbydion, pan vy waith Badbon
> > Arthur benn haclion y lasncu by gochion
> > Gwnaeth ar y alon gwaith gwyr gasynion
> > Gouynion gwacd darcdd mach deyrn ygogledd,
> > Heb d;ais heb d;ossedd.
>
> quæ in Latinum sermonem traducta ita exhibuit D. Johannes Priſæus:
>
> > O miseros illos nimiùm sub monte Badone
> > Quum cruor Arthuri, magnatum principis, ensem
> > Inficeret; susique foret jam sanguinis ultor
> > Heroum, quorum auxilio Borealia justè
> > Regna stetere diu.
>
> ic. ʳ Galfridus Monemuthensis prælii hujus historiam enarrans fusiùs, Sa
> 3,4. usque ad Sabrinum mare colonorum depopulatione

The fragmentary verse text, attributed to Taliesin, on Arthur and Mount Badon. The battle is here stated to be a quid pro quo for the Northern heroes who suffered in defence of their kingdoms.

> **Brytaines and Saxons.** 53
>
> ips at Tot- manes (as it is not vnlike) did build there in
> and burned times past.
> e hadde se-   Alla, and his 3 sons, Kimon, Plineing, and   Kingdome o
>   Cissa, came into Bytaine with three ships, and   the South
> ed Bing of landed with them, in a place called Kimenshore,   Saxons.
> ;itaines by and there slew many of the Bytaines, forcing   Marianus.
> nd courage the rest to make their flight into a wood called   Kimenshore
> s in which Andredsleage, this Alla fighting with the By-   Andredslea
> ent, calling taines in a place nerre vnto Mercreds Borne, or   Mercreds
> not for ever 10 Mercreds Rilear, slew many of them, & put the   borne.
> ; their cap- rest to flight.

Mearcraedesburn was a battle fought probably in Sussex, in the 480s. Arthur may have led the Britons. It remains unidentified. Here the 17th century Howe, building on the work of John Stow, indicates an added name of Rileur. This important site really ought to be identified soon. (I believe only carelessness has prevented this.)

A Tudor recreation of Camlan.

Here, at Moddershall (Modrede's Halh), in Staffordshire near Stone, perhaps Arthur's last battle was fought.

GILDAS. A FIFTEENTH-CENTURY STATUE AT LOCMINÉ

Gildas, the fiery 6th century ecclesiastic, whose surviving text on Britain is so important for our understanding of events.

These verses I haue the more willyngly inserted, for that I had the same deliuered to mee
turned into Englishe by maister Nicholas Ros-
carock, both right aptly yelding the sense, & also
properly aunswering the Latine, verse for verse.

VVho vanquisht Saxon troupes, with battayles
    bloudie broyles,
And purchaste to hymselfe a name with warlyke
    wealthie spoyles,
VVho hath with shiuering shining swordes, the
    Picts so oft dismayde,
And eke vnweldie seruile yoke on neck of Scots
    hath layde:
VVho Frenchmen pufft with pride, & who the
    Germaines fierce in fight
Discomfited, and daunted Danes with mayne
    and martiall might:
VVho of that murdring *Mordred* did the vitall
    breath expell,
That monster grisly, lothsom, huge, that diresom
    tyrant fell,
Here lyuelesse Arthur lies entombde, within this
    stately hearse,
Of chiualrie the brighte renoumie, and vertues
    nurslyng fierce:
VVhose glorie great, nowe ouer all the worlde,
    doth compasse flye,
And of the ayry thunder skales, the loftie buyl-
    ding hye.
Therfore you noble progenie of Brytayne lyne
    and race,
Aryse vnto your Emprour great, of thryce re-
    noumed grace,
And caste vpon his sacred tombe, the roseal gar-
    landes gaye,
That fragrant smell may witnesse well, your du-
    ties you display,

A 16th cent. Latin poem on Arthur by the antiquarian and keen Arthurian, John Leland, translated by the Tudor Nicholas Roscarrock, a Cornish enthusiast whose work on the Celtic saints was published recently for the first time.

This cross alleged to have been discovered at Glastonbury in 1191 7ft down, attached to a stone, under which lay the bones of Arthur and Gwenhwyfar, carries a suspicious Latin inscription. The cross is now lost.

This diagram shows the lettering on the 6th century Arthnou Stone found at Tintagel. Is the first element in the name simply a coincidence? Arthnou may scarcely postdate Arthur, for Arthur himself might have had a son living into the late 6th century.

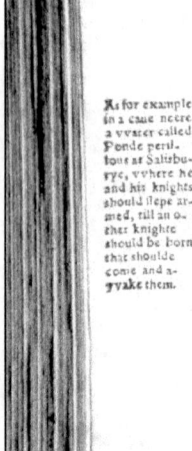

The Survival of Arthur. *The popular imagination did not allow Arthur to have died.*

King Arthur, as envisaged by a Tudor artist.

The Camp of Arthur, Huelgoat, northern Brittany.

The melody for Cian's Prophecy as recorded by La Villemarqué.

is, and doth consist, but these thinges came to passe in processe of time and yéeres.

Arthures round table.

Arthur hauing abated the rage of the Saxons as is afore shewed, and reduced his countrey to quietnesse, he constituted the order of the round table, into ỹ which order he onely retained such of his Nobility as were most renowned for vertue and Chiualrie. This round table he kept in diuers places, especially at Carlion, Winchester and Camalet in Somersetshyre. This Camalet

Camalet castle

sometime a famous towne, or castle standeth at the South end of the Church of south Cadbury, the same is situate on a very tor or hil, wonderfully strengthened by nature, to the which be 2. entrings vp, by very stéepe way, one by North, another by Southwest. The very rote of ỹ hill, whereon this fortresse stod, is more then a mile in compasse. In the vpper part of the top of the hill be 4. ditches or trenches, and a balky wal of earth betwixt euery one of them. In ỹ very top of the hill aboue all the trenches, is Magna area or campus, of 20. acres or more, wher in diuers places men may sée foundations, and rudor of wals. There was much duskie blew stone, that people of the village thereby hath carried away. This top within ỹ vpper wall being more then 20. acres, hath often béene plowed, + borne very good corne, much gold, siluer, and copper of the Romans coine hath bin found there in plowing, and likewise in the fields about the rotes of this hill, with many other antique thinges especially by East.

Leyland.

There was found in the memory of menne a horse shoe of siluer at Camalet. The people can tell nothing there but that they haue heard say, that Arthur much resorted to Camalet. The old Lord Hungarford was owner of this Camalet, since, Hasting Earle of Huntington by his mother, &c.

A 16th century description of South Cadbury Castle.

Chapter 14 - The Arthurian Peace

The next twenty years or so form the dream landscape in which the Arthurian romances are placed. It must have been a happy time for the Britons, with their hero of the resistance, Arthur, still amongst them.

We have no records of any warfare against foreigners in this period except in Sussex (on the south coast), where a group of Saxons arrived in 477 under their leader Aelle; and at an unknown site the first appearance of the future Wessex leaders in 495.

In 485, Aelle's men are recorded as fighting the Britons at Mearcraedesburn, a stream which appears to have formed a boundary subsequently.[*] Whether or not the Britons won this battle, a treaty was apparently concluded not only marking the limit of South Saxon territory but giving Aelle rule over Britons within his territory: that, at least, is what the title of 'Bretwalda' accorded to him suggests, though some believe it was only granted retrospectively, perhaps legitimizing later claims to it by other kings. His immediate successors did not have this title, nor is there proof that it was granted directly after Mearcraedesburn. But this battle bears witness to the kind of agreement between Britons and the newcomers, of which there are few traces.[*] Obviously, Arthur may have

---

[*] S.G Wildman proposes Glyndebourne: close by is Mark Cross. (Mark = mearc (border), ergo: border marker). He tentatively suggests that 3 miles off, the facing hillside turf memorials, the Long Man of Wilmington and the Ditchling Cross (the latter now no longer extant) are legacies of this event. Bosworth's *Mecreds Burnsted* appears to be a phantom, for Ethelwerd seems to have muddled the word for farmstead with that for bank (of a river).

led the British forces, but we do not know.

In 491, Aelle and his son Cissa besieged the Roman fort of Anderida, now Pevensey, on the south coast, massacring all its British inhabitants. But the outcome of this event is unknown. It would seem strange if the British had not retaliated to this outrage.

Another battle with which Arthur might be associated is recorded in an old Welsh poem on the death of Geraint, the son of king Erbin of Dumnonia. Geraint was father of Cadwy, whom we have already noticed in Cap.1. This battle may belong to the glory days before Badon, but, the enemy being unnamed, it is unclear. The poem can be traced in its present form to the early 9th century but is perhaps based on something much older.

… At Llongborth I saw[†] Arthur's
    brave men, they hewed with steel,
    [He] commander, leader in toil.
At Llongborth were slain Geraint's
    brave men from the lowlands of Devon,
    and before they were slain, they slew…

This fierce encounter, perhaps at Langport in Somerset[‡] a

---

[*] One is bound to think of Gildas' passage included at the end of the previous chapter. Aelle may have been a beneficiary of this wise and generous policy.

[†] Or, were slain.

[‡] Llamporth in Wales, on the coast near Pembryn, has a site, Beddgeraint - the grave of Geraint, so this must be seriously considered. I think the 'Portsmouth' death of a noble young Briton in the A-S Chronicle is too late, and unconnected. The Welsh site could indicate Irish settlers as the enemies.

few miles south of Glastonbury, shows Arthur and his men fighting beside Geraint. Other stanzas are devoted to their white steeds. This is a cavalry force, whose superiority over infantry was such that a Gallo-Roman, Ecdicius, about 470, routed Goths to the number of allegedly 4000 with some eighteen fellow-horsemen.

The word translated as 'commander' is ameraudur - derived from the Latin 'imperator'. Imperator might translate as either 'general' or 'emperor'. In Arthur's case, we need not doubt that the meaning was 'general', a title by which I suspect Arthur was customarily known in his own time. But, if Geoffrey misunderstood the title or took advantage of the double meaning, we have an explanation for Arthur being later identified as emperor.

The old genealogies generally give Geraint as a son of Erbin. But Erbin's father is given variously as Custennyn Gorneu (probably Gildas' Constantine) and Kynvawr (probably the tyrannical count of west Brittany, a model for Bluebeard, flourishing in the mid 6th century). This has led some to believe even that Geraint is the southern hero who lost his life at Catraeth (C.590), according to Aneirin. However, following another genealogy (in the Life of St Cybi) - which unfortunately manages to reverse Erbin and Gereint's father/son relationship - we find Erbin the son of an almost unknown Lud.[*]

This seems more plausible. For Geraint appears to be a genuinely Arthurian figure, and his son is recorded as Arthur's friend, and in Dumnonia, where Arthur was born, and, according to tradition, he spent his last days. In

---

[*] A Genealogy attached to the life of Winnoc has Riwal who came to settle in Brittany in the early 6th century descended from Cadwy, but is very muddled. Lud is probably Lludd of the Breastplate, a favourite of Arthur's court and battle-horseman (Triad 18w).

fact one may hypothesize at least three Geraints of Dumnonia - one from the early 8th century, and a late 6th and mid-5th century figure. And if the Geraint of Aneirin's were confused with the earlier one, we can see why Erbin's name was dragged in as well, that is, if the earlier Geraint were customarily known as 'son of Erbin'. Both Geraint and Cadwy are thought to have had saga cycles attached to their careers, and early sources place them both in relation to Arthur. I suggest that Geraint really did die fighting beside Arthur, to be replaced as ruler by his young son, who survived the campaigning, became a close friend of Arthur and died after a long and happy reign.*

Evidence is scant as always. In the 9th century Abbot Wrdisten of Landévennec refers to him as 'the most famous British king Catovius'. And in another saint's life of the 12th century St Carantoc is said to land in north Somerset [eastern Dumnonia] when 'Cato and Arthur ruled in that country, living in Dindraithou.'

The story that follows tells how Arthur confronts a terrible dragon at Carhampton. Carantoc subdues it, after which it is brought back to Dindraithou (= ? Dunster), and fed by Cato; there is a move to slay it but it is allowed to go free. In return, Arthur gives Carantoc land in Carhampton, his lost altar is restored to him (which Arthur had wanted to use as a table), and he builds a church there.

Behind this story there may be a wish to justify a claim on church land, of which Arthur obligingly puts his donation into a written document. The dragon motif is a regular occurrence in such literature. In the Breton life of

---

* He is named (i.e Cador) as father of Constantine, in Malory. But I think this is also mistaken.

St Efflam, Arthur pursues a dragon which he defeats with Efflam's help. The text reads '...the most powerful Arthur who at that time would seek out monsters in those parts of Brittany'. Perhaps this was how the early writers would characterize the marauders and brigands. We might compare Kleist's description of the hunt for the demonic Michael Kohlhaas: '[The governor] set out on holy St Gervasius' day to capture the dragon who was laying waste the countryside.'

These writers were story-tellers, and, perhaps behind others of Arthur's legendary adversaries including Twrch Trwyth (the tusk-boring pig) and Cath Paluc (the clawing cat), there are real historical figures ultimately lurking.

After all Sir Francis Drake has been a bogeyman for South American children for centuries; and children in my own immediate locality were threatened with the cannibal ogre, Cutty Dyer, even into the 20th century.

Two human adversaries are given by tradition, both probably from the period of the peace. One is Ligessauc Llawhir (long hand - meaning 'generous') son of Eliman, a brave leader who killed three of Arthur's men and had to flee for his life. He found refuge with St. Cadoc after relentless pursuit, and ultimately Cadoc mediated with Arthur for him.

Interesting as the story is, Ligessauc, whose name may be simply a description, 'Seafarer', is like his father without place or background. Frustratingly, we learn nothing about the nature of his opposition to Arthur's men.

A second opponent is altogether better defined. Hueil figures in a number of stories. He is characterized as brave and proud, recognizing allegiance to none. Late tradition has him taking possession of one of Arthur's mistresses leading to a fight and eventually his execution[*] by Arthur.

But in earlier literature, he stabs Gwydre son of Llwydeu, his own nephew. For some reason, Arthur cannot forgive this. Is Llwydeu related to Arthur? There is a Gwydre, Arthur's own son, in *Culhwch and Olwen*, slain by Twrch Trwyth at Cwm Cerwyn in Wales.

Another story of a son of Arthur whom Arthur killed is in the Historia Brittonum. The name of the son is given as Amr,[†] but this clearly refers to the river Gamber, by whose source (in Llanwarne) he is said to be buried. The site is said to be Wormelow Tump, sadly no more.

Since the compiler's immediately previous tale concerns the hunting of Twrch Trwyth by Arthur, it would not be difficult to imagine that he is telling a garbled version of the pig's killing Gwydre.[‡] And so Arthur's wrath at the stabbing of Gwydre - not Llwydeu's son but his own - would make sense.

Caradoc of Llancarfan, in his 12th century Life of Gildas, gives the fullest picture of Hueil: 'St. Gildas was the contemporary of Arthur, the king of the whole of Britain, whom he loved exceedingly, and whom he always desired to obey. Nevertheless his 23 brothers constantly rose up against the afore-mentioned warlike[14] king, refusing to own him as their lord, but they often routed

---

[*] The execution stone can be seen outside Barclays Bank on the market-square at Rhuthun. (R.Bromwich 1961)

[†] A son Amhar is mentioned as one of Arthur's chamberlains in mediaeval Welsh romance, but the reference is late and solitary.

[‡] For instance, the compiler might have read: 'He was a son of the soldier Arthur, and [while they were hunting Twrch Trwyth] *he* killed him there'. Then, omitting the bracketed passage, the compiler managed to muddle the true killer with Arthur.

and drove him out from forest and the battlefield. Hueil, the elder brother, an active warrior and most distinguished soldier, submitted to no king, not even to Arthur. He used to harass the latter, and to provoke the greatest anger between them both. He would often sweep down from Scotland, set up conflagrations, and carry off spoils with victory and renown. In consequence, the king of all Britain, on hearing that the high-spirited youth had done such things and was doing similar things, pursued the victorious and excellent youth, who, as the inhabitants used to assert and hope, was destined to become king. In the hostile pursuit and warrior gathering[*] held in the island of Minau (the Isle of Man), he killed the young plunderer. After that killing the victorious Arthur returned, rejoicing greatly that he had overcome his bravest enemy.'

There are a number of points one can make about this passage. First, we note that Hueil is called an elder brother of Gildas. Since Gildas was about 20 at the time of Arthur's death, his supposed brother, if from a large family, might be 20 years Gildas' senior, giving him an active career of up to 20 years before Arthur's death, and during the peace period.[†]

Hueil is a marauder from Scotland, responsible for conflagrations and plunder, and yet the tone of the author is not hostile, Arthur being characterized as warlike. It is also unclear what kingship the (Scottish?) inhabitants were

---

[*] I believe *bellicus conventus* is actually best translated as *armed parley*.

[†] Scholars are now inclined to disconnect Hueil from Gildas. But why should a Christianized Roman or Briton or Pict who came south not have an elder brother warrior, and not necessarily Christian , living in the north and marauding across borders as was the custom? Pictish converts had been known since the time of Ninian in the early 5th century.

hoping for Hueil.

A hostile pursuit by Arthur ends in a 'warrior gathering' on the Isle of Man leading to a fight in which Hueil is killed.

If there is any truth in this, and I believe there is, we have our best indication of the kind of opposition Arthur faced in peacetime: plundering opportunists raiding others' territories - and not excluding Britons - even if Gildas is happy to paint a rosy picture of British harmony at the beginning of his life.

The Irish Latin verses 'On an Attack', written probably in the early years of the 6th century, describe one such raid:[*]

... A certain rampaging band of armed brigands
approached the outer boundaries of an enemy land ...
[They killed, cooked and ate a boar]
... Then the native inhabitants of that land
busily began to fortify the outer boundaries of their native
    soil
Lest a hostile attack prevail over their ancestral
    ploughlands.

And now traversing the familiar bypaths of their
    boundary-land,
they espied the aforesaid band of brigands among the oaks
    of the forest.
Then the leafy woodland resounded with the onrushing
    horde,
and instantly the audacious troop cried out
that no survivors of their force would escape from the
    cruel slaughter

---

[*] Hisperica Famina.

before the savage claws of birds would bear them into the
    sky.
Next the raging leaders drew tight their battle lines
and turned their armed faces against the archers.
White stone is shot into the sky,
cruel darts penetrate alternately;
the aforesaid darts pierce meaty limbs,
and rivers of purple wind through fleshy flanks.
Enormous giants rush forward in battle
and sever round heads with their swords.
When the savage band of robbers broke the attacking
    phalanx with the strength of their fighting,
they stripped the dead bodies of their clothing
and heartlessly rejoiced with terrible shouts.
Then retreating to their home soil on a backward course
    the natives poured out a wealth of tales.'

These border raids were something of an institution, and Hueil was not despised but even praised for his high-spirited brand of free enterprise.[*]

---

[*] 'Wandering thieves with no taste for war' are the Romans' words from an earlier period, in Gildas cap. 18: in other words, marauders very difficult to catch up with who will flee on sight when faced with any serious opposition.

Chapter 15 - Continental Affairs 470-496

In France, Syagrius had ruled the 'kingdom' of Soissons since the murder of his father Aegidius in 464. Only the Angevin Chronicles note that he was raised to the throne by Romans *and* Goths. For the enemy, after a confused period, was now the Franks.

The success of campaigning against the Franks, in which we may suppose the Soissons Romans allied themselves with the Goths and Bretons, saw the Franks driven back to the Somme in the north-east. From here the Franks began a long blockade of Paris, of which the details are lost. We only know that St. Genevieve ran the blockade at some point to bring in fresh supplies by water from Arcis lying to the south-east.

But while the Franks were removed from the main field of conflict, the Goths grew more powerful, leading to Riothamus' intervention in 469. We cannot really imagine what the significance of a Gothic defeat would have been - most likely only temporary success for Bretons and Romans. The numbers of the incoming peoples were probably too great, and the long-term conclusion favouring the newcomers inevitable. Out of the intense rivalry between the main protagonists (if we exclude the Burgundians peacefully settled to the south) there may be a curious survival into modern times.

The French have a despised race called 'Cagots' of whose origins everyone appears to be in ignorance. But they have been mistreated horribly down the centuries as the gypsies were in our own country. My suggestion is that their name was originally Fran*ca-Go*t*hicus, and that they are descended from Frankish women unwise enough in those days to have relationships with Goths: at this point perhaps they and their descendants became hated outcasts of the Franks, as we have seen, for instance, in our own days the cruel attitude of many Norwegians to the unfortunate offspring resulting from a Nazi breeding programme involving Norwegian women in the last war. But in the early 470s, the Franks were struggling, and one might have favoured the Goths for Gallic supremacy. Brittany had had its share of raiders: Sidonius records devastation by Goths, Frisians and Saxons in the 450s, and the important north-west port of Brest, ruined by an invasion in 452, lost its bishopric for 50 years until the time of Ambrosius' presumed relation Paul Aurelian who transferred it elsewhere.

However, this was probably now a peaceful time. There is no evidence that the Goths capitalized on their victory at Déols except by consolidation, and it is quite probable that the Romans and Goths came to an accommodation of each other's interests. When Anthemius, besieged in Rome by Ricimer, sought help in 472, the general of the relief force appears to have been not a Briton nor Breton but a Goth, Bilimer - the help sadly tarnished by Bilimer's defection to Ricimer, after Bilimer had been defeated. Anthemius was discovered disguised as a beggar and killed. Three years later the emperor Julius Nepos ceded the region of the Auvergne to the Goths, of which they already had control.

For the Franks these were quiet years. They gave up the blockade C.475, and Childeric died six years later. His reign had been one of mixed fortune.[*] There was a tradition that his father Merovech was the son of a sea-

---

[*] His successes included the capture of Angers in 464; the capture of islands in the Loire from the Saxons; and the defeat of the Alamanni in Italy with Saxon help.

monster 'like a quinotaur' - a rumour of Merovech's mother's rape by a pirate? Childeric himself married the king of Thuringia's wife Bassina, she having deserted her own husband; it would seem that she was an old friend of his from his days in exile. Their son born in 465 was Clovis. He was sixteen at the time of his father's death, and an intensely ambitious young man.

His first target was Syagrius. He marched to Soissons in 486 and challenged him to combat. In the ensuing battle Syagrius' forces were routed,* and flight to the Gothic king Alaric II (who had recently succeeded Euric) in Toulouse did not save him. Alaric browbeaten by Clovis handed Syagrius over bound to him: he imprisoned Syagrius and had him secretly executed after securing Soissons.

Clovis' long string of triumphs in the coming years included his defeat of the Thuringians in 491, and of other Frankish chieftains, though not the Goths with whom he was at peace. But he could not defeat the Bretons despite capturing Blois.

A state of war persisted until a tentative treaty was signed in 491. Then in 497 the two sides drew up a final accord in which the Bretons and Armoricans were exempted from paying tribute and granted a limited autonomy and certain new territory: the Bretons were required to recognize Frankish supremacy, maintain an alliance and desist from the use of the title of king; Clovis' conversion to Christianity was probably also a condition of the agreement. This was the beginning of Brittany's unusual status within France; their semi-independence such that full independence, (achieved in the 9th century

---

* Syagrius did not fear to fight him. Nor was the result a foregone conclusion. The king of the Salian Franks stood on the sidelines awaiting the outcome.

and not altogether lost until 1514), has been a matter of continuing debate, and sometimes action even into modern times.

One follower of Arthur's may be associated with these events. Lancelot, a main figure in the romances, is evidently a foreigner, coming out of Breton, and not British tradition. His father is named as King Ban of Benwick, whose brother is Bors of Gaul. These brothers are at war with King 'Claudas' whom they much fear.

Might these not be Bretons in the tempestuous years between the beginning of Clovis' (Chlodoveus') reign in 481, and the settled peace of 497? In Malory's time, some believed Benwick to be Bayonne, some Beaune, but these were surely guesses.

If we place Benwick in Brittany, we can see why a secondary figure in Arthur's story might have been seized upon by French and especially Breton romances, because he was one of their own. However nothing can yet be resolved with any confidence relative to this deeply obscure figure.[*]

---

[*] Banw and Benwig are slain by Twrch Trwyth, in *Culhwch and Olwen*, just after Twrch *Llawin* is. This is presumably a coincidence because Llawin is on the side of Twrch Trwyth. See also Appendix: Lancelot.

Chapter 16 - Arthur's Friends and Relatives

We have seen Arthur arrive, into the last period of his life, that is post-Badon. He is now well into his fifties: his old friends Cei and Bedwyr (Kay and Bedivere) are with him still, his foster-brother and their mutual friend from days of long ago, together over more than forty successful and exciting years. The older generation are most probably dead - Arthur's mother, Eigr (Igerna) and Cei's parents who fostered Arthur. We know nothing of what happened to Leonora after he deserted her for Gwenhwyfar. Loholt was said to be their son, and elsewhere Borre: if there is any truth in the Glastonbury epitaph (or epitaphs)* she was married to him, it would seem. But as Cei appears to have been her brother, and he and Arthur did not at that time become enemies, perhaps this ended as amicably as such things may.

I have mentioned Arthur's likely links with Ambrosius,† (dead C.470?) and Aegidius (murdered 464). His second wife Gwenhwyfar's father Ogyrfan whom Arthur is said in the Romances to have aided against King Ryons (see Appendix), also fades from the story. His kingdom may have been short-lived, perhaps swallowed up in the territorial conquests of Maelgwn Gwynedd, an ambitious North Welsh king of the late 5th and early 6th centuries. Ogyrfan's son and successor might be the Yvain of Cavaliot mentioned in an ancient list of Arthur's

---

* See Cap 18.

† A possibly 10th century poem links Cei and Ambrosius: 'Before the lords of Emrys I saw Cei in haste': This might suggest that Cei (and Arthur) led Ambrosius' allies after Ambrosius' death or even before.

followers.*

Chief amongst Arthur's private entourage - his *army* is probably the best description - excluding Cei, Bedwyr and the mysterious Lancelot, are Gwalchmei and Caradawc Vreichvras.[†]

Gwalchmei we have already seen expelled by the Saxons from his northern kingdom probably in the 460s: he was said to be Arthur's sister's son, the sister having married a Scottish or Pictish king. Gwalchmei is Gawain in the romances (through a derivation from the Latin form of his name), 'a paragon of valour and courtesy', as Rachel Bromwich describes him.

But Caradawc Vreichvras or 'Strong Arm' seems to have been of an earlier generation. He is associated in Welsh tradition with the foundation of the dynasty that ruled Glamorgan in Wales. He is also linked with a kingdom in Brittany,[‡] possibly Vannes,[§] but this is hardly credible. The Bretons did not take Vannes out of Gallo-Roman control till 580. Like Rennes and Nantes, it long remained an important independent enclave. So, realistically, Caradawc's Breton territory is uncertain.

However, it is as Arthur's senior counsellor that we take most interest in Caradawc, for he is thus described in

---

* Chrétien de Troyes, *Eric et Enide*.

[†] It is needless to attempt to list lesser members of the entourage such as the Chieftains given in Triad 9, who as Mike Ashley suggests, by their very obscurity, might be genuine Arthurian figures. Rahawd son of Morgant might just rate a mention. Famed as a lover, this peer of Arthur's court won renown also as a frivolous bard, perhaps vying with Arthur.

[‡] Life of St Padarn.

[§] Livre de Carados.

the (Welsh) *Dream of Rhonabwy*. Elsewhere in the Triads, he is one of the three battle-horsemen[15], and one of the three favourites of Arthur's court.* An important figure, then, though his achievements remain unknown to us.

There is little to tell about Arthur's son, Llacheu, who nevertheless appears to have had a significant place in the early Welsh tradition. In one early allusion, he 'makes slaughter' with Cei[16]. But it is for his death he is generally remembered, which is supposed to have happened 'below Llech Ysgar', perhaps a court in Powys.

The Romances refer to a son, Loholt, whom some consider distinct from Llacheu. It seems reasonable to take Loholt as some kind of misunderstood description (e.g. Llaw hallt, from the Welsh, or a French expression derived from *haut*). But Loholt of the Romances is a minor character, and we learn nothing new. He is named by separate sources as son of Guinevere, and again of Lissanor (=Leonora).

Galahad, son of Lancelot, is even more obscure than his father. Generally considered to be entirely a mediaeval invention (his name being derived from the Biblical Mount Gilead), he nevertheless bears a name very similar to one of Arthur's followers in *Culhwch and Olwen*, Gwalhafed, named as a brother of Gwalchmei. So it would not be altogether unreasonable to suggest that a more or less forgotten follower, Arthur's own nephew, was 'rediscovered' centuries later, though our evidence does not support this. Remarkably he stole the show from the older heroes, and, alone amongst them, Sir Galahad has become proverbial, for chivalry and gallantry.

It would be pleasing to see in the name of Brastias (also Bractias), a minor follower of Arthur's in the

---

* Triads 18 and 18W.

romances, a derivation from 'ab Riagath', i.e son of Riocatus. Riocatus - actually, 'Briacat' - is named in the Historia Brittonum as son of that Pascent who was generously treated by Ambrosius after his father Vortigern's death.[*] He was a priest in an amusing story told by Sidonius who was Riocatus' friend: Riocatus' party is waylaid by Sidonius' men after leaving the bishop: Sidonius wants to see and copy a manuscript that he has got wind of, amongst Riocatus' baggage.

If Riocatus' son (possibly Idnerth) were recorded as Briocatus or Briagath, this might offer a direct connexion between Vortigern's dynasty and Arthur. But I confess this as a fond rather than probable speculation: Brastias latterly turns to religion and becomes a hermit.

A certainly historical figure is Ewein Danwyn, Ewein 'Whiteteeth', grandson of Cunedda. After Ewein's brother Cadwallawn Llawhir's death, Maelgwn, son of Cadwallawn, in a successful attempt to enlarge his north Welsh territory attacked his surviving uncle.

Amongst the many sins and crimes committed by Maelgwn, Gildas takes note in a tirade of this episode: 'Did you not in the beginning of your youth most fiercely oppress the king your uncle and his bravest warriors as it were - whose features in battle much resembled those of young lions - with sword, spear and fire?'

Ewein lost his kingdom and perhaps at the same time his life, and this must have happened in the 490s or 500s. For Maelgwn died in 547 after a long and tumultuous life, his death even being commemorated in a proverb: 'The

---

[*] Pascent is possibly commemorated by Pontesbury, formerly *Posentes byrg*, near Shrewsbury. His Roman name was shared with an early 5th century Christian heretic.

long sleep of Maelgwn in the court of Rhos'.

Though there is no Ewein Whiteteeth in the romances - despite the presence of at least two Uwaines, (a derivation from the Roman Eugenius, 'high-born', and now found as Owen) - we find Uwaine (or Ewaine) le Blanchemains, that is Ewein Whitehands. He is the son of king Uriens of Gore and stepson of Arthur's sister, Morgana. Gore is Gower in South Wales.

Now the much more reliable genealogies name Ewein Danwyn's father as Enniaun Yrth, whose kingdom was in North Wales, if we assume that Ewein Danwyn inherited it. But isn't it possible that Ewein Whiteteeth and Ewein Whitehands are one and the same, with an error in the romance parentage? (And it would be ludicrous to suggest that a sister of Arthur's married Enniaun Yrth).

If so, Ewein is found to be a relative of Arthur's as follows:

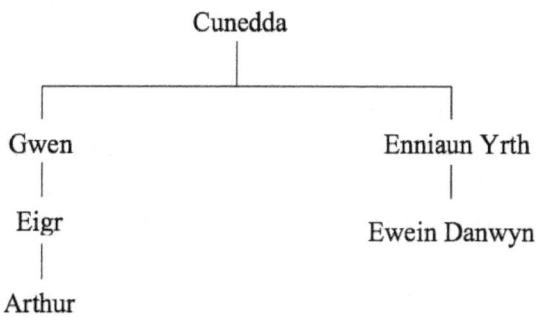

There is nothing inherently unlikely in Maelgwn's uncle, the recipient of Gildas' discreet praise and evidently a good man, following his cousin as a companion soldier into the wars.

Arthur's first cousin Illtud, son of Arthur's maternal aunt Rienguleid and a Breton warrior, Bican (whose father is named as Kenais on the authority of the dubious Iolo

Mss), is recorded as crossing from Brittany to Britain, probably in the 450s. Arriving in the south-west, he headed for the court of his cousin: '… Here he saw a very great company of soldiers, being also honourably received in that place, and being rewarded as regards his military desire. His desire to receive gifts being also satisfied, he withdrew very pleased…'

So, armed with gifts and a military commission or letter of recommendation, he travelled on to Poulentus, a king of Glamorgan and became master of the soldiers in due course.[*]

The meeting with Arthur - if it was a meeting with Arthur in person - has been doubted. But there is nothing incredible. The receiving of a commission may have been the main purpose of his visit. There may be a suggestion that Illtud had not seen his cousin for many years. Arthur is recorded, in the Triads, as having a court in Cornwall at an unidentified Celli Wig, and this is the most likely setting for their encounter.[†]

After Illtud's spell as master of the soldiers, he went into the church, having put away his wife, embarking on a long and hugely successful career as one of the earliest of the Celtic Saints, or holy men. Based at his monastery at Llantwit Major, he was a teacher to many, including St.

---

[*] Poulentus recognized him as a 'court' soldier, and, while treated honourably and well, Illtud was not given his office as magister militum for some time. The writer hardly makes the most of Illtud's visit to Arthur's court, neither identifying the setting nor including any anecdote or dialogue between Illtud and Arthur, leaving in doubt whether Arthur was actually present.

[†] This was early in Arthur's career. His wealthy family must have had land in western Dumnonia, where his mother probably still lived.

David and King Maelgwn.[*]

The late 12th century *Lay of Eliduc*, by the gifted writer, Marie de France, composing for a courtly audience, tells of another well-born Breton crossing the sea to the south-west: Eliduc arrived at the court of an old king near Exeter, to whom he rendered successfully military aid. *The king's delight extended to his appointing Eliduc Seneschal and Constable of his realm.*

Eliduc fell in love with the king's daughter, Guillardun, as she did with him. But Eliduc already had a Breton wife. The upshot was that the king's daughter discovered he was married, and his wife learned about her rival. *But magnanimously his wife accepted the situation and elected to become a nun. He built a church and a convent for her.*

The stories of Illtud and Eliduc have a number of features in common.

A well-born Breton crosses to
   the south-west.
He becomes master of soldiers
   of an old[†] king.
He puts his wife away, and
   she becomes a nun.
He builds a church.

Even Eliduc's name is reminiscent, forms such as Eltut(us) and Hildut(us) being not known for Illtud.

There are many differences in these stories too, but,

---

[*] '... you have had as your teacher the refined master of almost all Britain ...' (Gildas).

[†] Poulentus may be Poul Hen (Old Paul) Latinized. He is Paul (of) Pennichen, uncle of Cadoc and brother of Cadoc's father, Gundleius. (see Cap. 19)

coincidence or otherwise, Illtud was perhaps following what became a tried and familiar path in choosing a career overseas, and turning latterly to the Church.

Arthur's sister Morgana has been mentioned already as well as another sister who married a Pictish king and was mother to Gwalchmei. Malory gives Margawse as her name, while she is generally recorded as Gwyar if that is not her husband's name. A third, Elaine, is wife of king Nentres of Garlot, renowned for her beauty as Morgana for learning. All are deeply obscure figures.

The beautiful Elaine's (Helena's) kingdom Garlot reminds one of Gwrgi *Garwlwyd* (= rough-grey, perhaps with reference to his being a werewolf), Bedwyr's opponent at the battle of Tribruit. But it is hard to see why Gwrgi should be an enemy if he comes from the same region or even family. Tentatively one might place Garlot in the north.

Margawse (also Morgawse) or Gwyar (who might however be Gwalchmei's father) is a more solid figure because of her son. A Pictish or Scottish alliance would have been very useful to Arthur, and Arthur's battles seemingly fought in the north must have involved warriors from his sister's kingdom if it survived his nephew's expulsion. But our northern information is ridiculously slight despite the continuing existence of the British kingdom of Strathclyde in Southern Scotland, and for many centuries afterwards.[*]

Morgana is the subject of story far more than the other two, and remains the most vivid of the three. But

---

[*] St Patrick's letter of complaint to King Coroticus is probably from the 450s, only shortly before Arthur was in action in Britain. But Coroticus was not necessarily king of Strathclyde. See Supplementary Note for another possibility[16].

whether she should be treated as flesh and blood or simply an enigma is open to question. Malory tells us: '... the third sister, Morgan le Fay, was put to school in a nunnery: and there she learned so much that she was a great clerk of nigromancy. And after she was wedded to king Uriens of the land of Gore, that was Sir Ewaine's le Blanchemains father ...'

The 12th century romancer Chrétien de Troyes adds: 'Graislemier of Fine Posterne ... had with him his brother Guigomar, lord of the isle of Avalon.

...we have heard it said that he [Guigomar] was a friend of Morgan the Fay, and such he was ...'

In the lays of Marie de France from the same period, Gugemar falls in love with a beautiful, unnamed lady who deserts her elderly, jealous husband, a king, to be with him.

But a confusion between Morgan le Fay and the Celtic goddess Modron seems irresoluble. In the early 13th century, Giraldus Cambrensis clearly substitutes Morgan for the goddess. At best, one can suggest that a sister of Arthur's was subsequently identified with the goddess either because she was a matrona (matron), or because she is said to have healed Arthur after his last battle as a goddess might do. She has her own curious little memorial in the aerial phenomenon seen in the Straits of Messina off Sicily known as the Fata Morgana.* This probably dates from the time of Breton storytellers following their Norman masters into Sicily after its conquest in 1194.

---

* The Irish water-spirit 'Morrigan' is obviously connected.

Chapter 17 - Camlan: Why and Where

'The battle of Camlann in which Arthur and Medraut fell …'

(Annales Cambriae)

The Arthurian peace had lasted for nearly two generations at the time when Gildas wrote C.520. And for the first twenty years or so that saw Gildas into manhood, Arthur himself was present. His life was ended by a bitter row, so far as we can tell, but there is no certainty what the dispute was about.

We have seen a number of events where talk turned to violence: Ambrosius' confrontation with Vitalinus in 436 would be one example. Here the fighting was light: the battle was no more than a skirmish (*discordia*), and we are most probably witnessing a savage *political* rupture.

The massacre of the Concilium was of course a gross act of treachery, for both sides were supposed to attend unarmed.

The killing of Hueil in a 'warrior gathering' on the Isle of Man is another example. A parley turned into fighting, probably after an attempt at a peaceful settlement.

Mearcraedesburn in 485 was a battle probably ending in a stalemate and perhaps followed immediately by a peace conference, reversing the usual process.

The mid-6th century poet Taliesin thus recounts a later confrontation preceding the battle of Argoed Llwyfain. The enemy is an unknown Saxon, Fflamddwyn:

… Fflamddwyn hollered
  with great commotion:
    have my hostages come,
    are they ready?

And answered Owain,
  the scourge of the east,
- They haven't come,
They don't exist,
They aren't ready, -
And the whelp of Coel
would be a pathetic warrior
before he would pay anybody
  a hostage.

Urien,
Lord of Erechwydd,
shouted:
If there's to be a meeting
  for a parley,
let's raise our banners
  above the mountain,
let's lift our faces up
  to the edge,
let's raise our spears above
  the heads of men
and make for Flamddwyn
  and his followers ...[*]

The parley, usually with weapons, was a convention that might prevent bloodshed. But the mood of both sides would not always be conducive to a peaceful ending.[†]

Arthur's opponent in the dispute is named as Medraut, though his opposition is not clear in the Annales Cambriae. He was very probably the grandson of Arthur's

---

[*] Taliesin - Poems - trans. Meirion Pennar - Llanerch, 1988.

[†] See Appendix: The Raid of the Reidswire.

counsellor, Caradawc Strong Arm, and son of one of the holy men of the period: he would be much younger than Arthur.[*]

Though the Welsh poets make many references both to him and Arthur's final battle, in which they are much more interested than Mount Badon, their allusions make little sense to us.

'Three Harmful Blows of
 the Island of Britain:
 ... The second Gwenhwyfach
struck upon Gwenhwyfar: and
for that cause there took
place afterwards the Action
of the Battle of Camlan...'
(Triad 53)

'Three Unrestrained Ravagings
 of the Island of Britain:

The first of them (occurred) when Medrawd came to Arthur's Court at Celliwig in Cornwall; he left food nor drink in the court that he did not consume. And he dragged Gwenhwyfar from her royal chair, and then he struck a blow upon her;

The second ... (occurred) when Arthur came to Medrawd's court. He left neither food nor drink in the court ...'

(Triad 54)

'Three Futile Battles of
 the Island of Britain:

---

[*] His son is also named as a saint. Morris connects him with Dunwich, in Suffolk.

> ... And the third was the
> worst: that was Camlan,
> which was brought about
> because of a quarrel between
> Gwenhwyfar and Gwenhwy(f)ach'
> (Triad 84)

A late poet, William Llŷn, makes Gwenhwyfar responsible: 'There was a sad slaughter, provoked by wanton passion, Camlan through slaughter and pursuit; and fair Gwenhwyfar, lively-nurtured, yellow-haired, brought it about.'[17]

In *Culhwch and Olwen*, we find Gwyn the Irascible, overseer of Devon and Cornwall, one of the nine who plotted Camlan. If he is the same as Gwyn, son of Ermid, son of Erbin also mentioned, Gwyn becomes King Cadwy's first cousin, adding credence to the possibility of his involvement. Gwenhwyfach is named as a sister of Gwenhwyfar.[*]

We may also mention, in the mediaeval Welsh romance, *The Dream of Rhonabwy*, that someone called Iddawg son of Mynio (elsewhere Iddawg is named as Medraut's brother) admits to the nickname, Embroiler of Britain. For he was an envoy at Camlan and distorted messages deliberately that were sent from Arthur to Medraut. Here Arthur is referred to as foster-father and uncle of Medraut, and one may suspect Geoffrey's influence, though he never mentions Iddawg.

Hazarding a guess based on the evidence here presented, I suggest that Gwenhwyfar was a somewhat flighty woman whose tendencies were enhanced by her

---

[*] Medraut's name seems to lurk behind the (jocular) Gwenhwyfach, as Sir Ifor Williams proved in one instance.

husband's frequent absences, and that Medraut was one of her young lovers.*

There is a story of Melvas, a ruler in eastern Dumnonia (Somerset), in which he is said to have abducted her for a year; but perhaps she was not altogether unwilling, as the poets have a tradition of great passion between them[18].

But, deeply troubled by her inconsistency or rebuffs, Medraut lost his temper at Celliwig when she was present without her husband. Medraut wounded in his heart even went so far as striking her - much as the earl of Essex famously boxed the ears of Queen Elizabeth I.

Arthur was furious when he heard, and demanded an apology from Medraut, which the hot-headed young man mistakenly refused to give.† For the honour of his lady, Arthur called his men to arms…..

Medraut was young and the grandson of Arthur's old friend and fellow-soldier. He is also recorded by the poets as a paragon of chivalry and virtue, as we might expect if his father was a saint. Arthur probably had the kindliest feelings towards him, and one may suspect Medraut was a regular guest at Celliwig. But something had to be done, for Gwenhwyfar was in great distress, or, more likely, a rage. By a show of strength the matter could still be settled peacefully.

If what precedes seems like a ridiculous fantasy,

---

* In Malory, Medraut tries to marry her, while Geoffrey tells us: '[Medraut] was living adulterously and out of wedlock with… Guinevere who had broken the vows of her earlier marriage. About this … Geoffrey … prefers to say nothing.' If the son of Medraut's mentioned earlier is legitimate, we should think of Medraut as married like Gwenhwyfar.

† This might explain Arthur's visit, in Triad 54.

remember the triangular nature of the event - an older married man and a youngish man in opposition, and the married man's wife held to blame or at the very least deeply involved. The Annales entry might allow Arthur and Medraut on the same side, but this is less likely, being in defiance of the whole tradition.

Arthur and his troops went in search of Medraut. But where? Medraut had left Cornwall (in which there are still traces of his erstwhile presence) and travelled some distance out of Dumnonia. For there are no sites in the south-west called Camlan nor do we have reason to believe there ever were.[*]

The name Camlan(n) tells us a little: it is a compound of two Brythonic words: *Cambo* - crooked, and either *glanna* - bank or shore, or *landa* - probably moor or heath, though via its Welsh and Breton derivatives it developed into 'enclosure'. We are looking for a patch of rough ground distinguished by a curve, or ground encircled by a bending river. No one is now convinced by Geoffrey's attempt to place it near Camelford in Cornwall; he Latinizes the river Camel there as Cambla (n).

We believe from ancient sources that the fort of Castlesteads on Hadrian's Wall was formerly Camboglanna. But this is a long way north for two Dumnonians to go, and no traditions of the battle relate to it, though Sewingshields Farm to the east figures, if differently, in Arthurian legends.

There is a detailed story how Arthur and his men

---

[*] Tedion Modredis Sunu is found in the Bodmin manumissions of the late 10th century; Carveddras (formerly Kaervodred) is in Kenwyn, near Truro; and Tremodrett near Roche is found as Tremodret in the Domesday Book. Rosemodrass near Boleigh is also a possibility. Of course, one cannot prove these are all references to the same person.

were travelling from the fort of Dinas Emrys, trying to reach the pass at Cwm Tregalan in Snowdonia. He met the enemy at Cwm Llan and drove them back. But he ran into an ambush by archers, was killed, and was buried where he fell at a cairn called Carnedd Arthur still extant in the 18th century. The Welsh name of the pass still carries the meaning "the pass of the Arrows." Nearby is "The Cave of the young Men," where those who survived Camlan are said to be sleeping.*

It is impossible to know how ancient this interesting tradition is. But Cwm Llan is not Camlan, and it would be surprising if within Welsh territory Camlan had subsequently lost its name.

Much more intriguing is Camlan near Mallwyd in Merioneth. A man called Osfran's son is said in a verse of an old Welsh poet to be buried at the battle site. Patrick Sims-Williams points out that there is a vague reference to the otherwise unknown Osfran in a 12th century poem praising St. Cadfan and his church at Tywyn only about eighteen miles from the Mallwyd site. (A dozen miles to the north is Bala Lake beside which Arthur's foster-family lived.)[19]

This is perhaps our most likely site, but there is no gauging how many other Camlans, in territory subsequently conquered by the Saxons, lost their names. Our traditions about Camlan lack precision. The Cwm Llan story is not only spoiled by lack of a Camlan but by "Arthur's Cairn" itself, which ought not to have been there, since his burial-place was a great mystery.

I shall venture one more site, one that has not yet

---

* I take most of these details from F.J Snell. The legend is recorded in Y Brython.

Camlan: Why and Where | 115

received consideration. Five miles to the north-east of Stone, a small town in Staffordshire, and lying about thirty miles east of the old Roman city of Viroconium repaired in the late 5th century by some unknown chieftain, is the sleepy, sloping little village of Moddershall.

In the Domesday Book, this is to be found as Modredeshale, derived from Modred's Halh. The strong resemblance to Medraut's name - remember the Cornish forms, Modredis and Modret - encourages the belief that he is genuinely being referred to, and this is wholly surprising in what became Saxon territory. Perhaps we should consider the possibility that he was a friend of settlers in those parts, even an ally.

Ekwall distinguishes a wide variety of related meanings for *halh*: 'a corner, angle, a retired or secret place, cave, closet, recess'; in the South and Midlands, it usually seems to be, 'a nook, recess, remote valley'; in the North it developed a special meaning viz, 'haugh', a piece of flat alluvial land by the side of a river, and he refers to an intermediate sense: 'land in a corner formed by a bend.'

Away from the hills, the village offers a gentle incline across pasture land down to the confluence of two streams. Close to this confluence we find a table-flat surface of land on a bend, close to the remains of a mill, fitting Ekwall's intermediate sense particularly well (and a name beginning *Cambo*), though it must be confessed that Staffordshire is in the Midlands, not the North.

The preservation of Medraut's name is extraordinary: Did he live there? Did he run a mill? Why should his memory be commemorated so far from Western Dumnonia? Or is the name a Saxon's? Or simply another British Medraut whom only the Saxons have recorded?

It is perhaps no more than a fancy that Medraut left (fled?) Cornwall and returned to a place with which he had long been familiar; and here Arthur found him; and the battle was fought around the watercourses, in this pleasantly atmospheric little spot. (There is no record of where Medraut lies buried.)[*]

---

[*] For those who doubt Arthur at 72 taking part, this is the same age as Blucher rescuing Europe, with his late arrival at Waterloo, from Napoleon. In the prophetic section of Geoffrey's book, we find in old translations that two kings will fight over a lioness near Stafford. (Moddershall is near Stafford). Alas! The Latin pretty clearly indicates a lioness *of* Stafford. (de vado baculi)

Chapter 18 - The Battle of Camlan and Arthur's Grave

The only likely detail of the battle itself is the statement in a Triad:

'Three unfortunate Counsels of the Island of Britain...
    and the third: the three-fold dividing by Arthur of his men with Medrawd at Camlan.' (Triad 59)

This has been understood as a chivalrous act but appears almost incomprehensible. If Arthur's force were much larger than Medraut's, he might have compromised his advantage. This would be a remarkable act of respect to his opponent, but it is surely the stuff of romance literature sooner than a truth preserved by the old Welsh tradition.[*] Malory's story is of Medraut as a traitor and usurper. It is taken from Geoffrey. But his finale is distinct: a treaty is arrived at but the parties agree that Arthur and Medraut shall meet, each with fourteen men, in yet another armed parley. However, one of the soldiers is bitten at the meeting by an adder and, not thinking, draws his sword. This ends the hope of a peaceful conclusion.

In the ensuing fight Arthur is severely wounded and taken away by barge. Amongst the women who attend are three queens including his sister Morgana, but not Gwenhwyfar. Their objective is to take him for healing to the Vale of Avilion.

Outside the pages of Malory there are one or two old

---

[*] In the triad, if we add the words 'before fighting' after 'men', we have a straightforward strategic error: Arthur wrongly subdivided his troops.

lists of alleged survivors. Morfran son of Tegid is one; he becomes interesting for his association with Llyn Tegid (Bala Lake), so close to one of our suggested settings for the battle. If he were also linked with Os*fran*, he would be even more interesting, since Osfran's son was buried at Camlan.*

Faithful Bedwyr, whom the romances place at the last battle (and immortalized by his failure to obey Arthur's instructions to throw Excalibur into the water) is recorded as being buried on Tryvan, a peak in Snowdonia. As he is mentioned in the same verse as Osfran's son, this may be a small additional confirmation of his presence at the battle.†

Saint Petrock, who must have been very young, is also said to have been present. 'Precious Petrock was renowned with his weapon at the death of Arthur.'‡ He was known as Paladrddellt i.e. Splintered-Spear. At Llanbedrog in Caernarvonshire his spear was exhibited, in 1535. It was described as a 'Relyk called Gwawe Pedrock', according to the parish rector. It is possible to doubt how old the tradition of Petrock's participation really is; but let us not dismiss it. (If Bedwyr son of Bedrawc were

---

* If we substitute Ogvran for Ossvran in the original text, we find a brother of Gwenhwyfar's.

† Llywelyn ap y Moel, a mediaeval poet, claimed that Cei was heart-broken after Bedwyr's death, his misery finding voice in a terrible cry. The romances have Bedwyr becoming a hermit after Camlan, as also they have Gwenhwyfar becoming a nun in Amesbury (Wiltshire). Cei, the last survivor of the 3 warrior friends, was thought by Iolo Morgannwg to have been buried at Cai Hir (= Tall Cei (as he was known)) at Aberavan in Glamorganshire.

‡ Dafydd Nanmor.

recorded as a survivor, this would *sound* very like Bedwyr and Petrock, in Welsh)

Gwalchmei was not present, according to the romances. In the early 12th century, William of Malmesbury tells us this:

'At this time [i.e. 1066 -1087] was found in the province of Wales called Rhos the tomb of Walwen [Gwalchmei]... A warrior most renowned for his valour, he was expelled from his kingdom by the brother and nephew of Hengest... but not until he had compensated for his exile by much damage wrought upon them, worthily sharing the praise of his uncle, in that they deferred for many years the ruin of their falling country. But the tomb of Arthur is nowhere to be beheld, whence ancient ditties fable that he is yet to come. The tomb of the other, however, as I said, was found in the time of King William upon the sea-shore, fourteen feet in length; and here some say that he was wounded by his foes and cast out in a shipwreck, but according to others he was killed by his fellow citizens at a public banquet. Knowledge of the truth therefore remains doubtful, although neither story would be inconsistent with the defence of his fame.'

The story of his being wounded and cast out in a shipwreck has its echo in Malory: Medraut tries during his period of treachery to stop Arthur landing at Dover from the Continent. There is a great naval battle in which Medraut's forces are defeated.

'So when this battle was done, king Arthur let bury his people that were dead, and then was the noble knight Sir Gawaine found in a great boat, lying more than half dead.' Geoffrey's story has Gawain dying as he and Arthur attempt to land at Richborough. So, though Geoffrey may have taken the detail from William, it looks as if there was a genuine tradition involving Gwalchmei's being wounded at sea.*

In an early Welsh poem Gwalchmei appears to have been buried beside a stream running into the Monnow at Monmouth. The poet refers to the grave as 'a reproach to men', clearly seeing the death as shameful and probably favouring the banquet story. (The burial site Peryddon might be not the stream but Periton south of Minehead in Somerset.) The stream Periron mentioned twice by Geoffrey is probably the same. But this does not appear to be in Rhos, where however one of the three commotes is called Kastell Gwalchmei, Gwalchmei's Castle. Finally a more modern source records that Gwalchmei's grave was shown between the islands of Skomar and Skokham off Pembrokeshire, where also Rhos is.†

Evidently the waters on the coast of Rhos had withdrawn abnormally for the tomb to surface; or a storm had cleared sand away to reveal it at depth. And with the constantly changing coastline it may be that we must now look for Gwalchmei's tomb under the sea.

It is a feature of the lives of those in great favour with their contemporaries that we are unwilling to believe them dead despite overwhelming contrary evidence. And so it was with Arthur, though we cannot say whether this *fever* was immediate. He died in the battle or very shortly afterwards - our best source, the Annales Cambriae,

---

* It cannot be ruled out that Gwalchmei's death postdated Camlan, and that the romances have simply followed Geoffrey in placing the death earlier.

† The 10th century Armes Prydein refers to Aber Peryddon, a town at the river mouth probably in south-eastern Wales. It is unclear how Gwalchmai on Anglesey, with Trearddur Bay to the west, relates to him if at all, for there was an early mediaeval Anglesey poet of the same name.

favouring death in battle[20].

But where was he buried? Such an illustrious warrior, the greatest general of his time and hero of the resistance, would surely find an honoured resting-place. While his wife Gwenhwyfar would probably have the ultimate decision, surely Cadwy his friend and king would also have his say - though it cannot be denied that Arthur might have expressed his own wishes.

Three possible destinations suggest themselves: Celliwig in western Dumnonia (Cornwall), a stronghold of his though sadly unidentified; the great Abbey at Glastonbury which one would expect to have been Cadwy's choice; and another of his strongholds believed to be one near Glastonbury, in eastern Dumnonia.

This stronghold is Cadbury Castle at South Cadbury about which there have been Arthurian traditions for centuries. John Leland, the early 16th century antiquary, gives the following description: 'At the very south ende of the church of South-Cadbyri standith Camallate, sumtyme a famose toun or castelle, apon a very torre or hille, wunderfully enstrengtheid of nature... The people can telle nothing ther but that they have hard say that Arture much resortid to Camalat.' The Welsh antiquary, Elis Gruffudd, of nearly the same date says: [The English] 'in their opinion say that he is asleep in a cave under a hill near Glastonbury.' The castle is eleven miles away.

This massive hill-fort, then, is identified with the Camelot of the romances: there is no Camelot recorded till the time of Chrétien de Troyes in the latter 12th century. Because of a strong tradition, we must respect the possibility that it is accurate. It would be natural to expect Arthur in peacetime, if not before, to have a base in eastern Dumnonia, both to protect the borders and to be near his friend the king with whom we have found him closely associated, one of the king's palaces being surely located close to Glastonbury[21].

Furthermore, it may be possible to explain the name. For, a very short distance westward lie the Camels, Queen Camel and West Camel, their names deriving from two British words, cant - rim(?) and moel - bare, meaning something like 'the bare-rimmed hills'.

If an English guide had taken French visitors to Cadbury, might they not have asked the name of Arthur's castle in the form of "Where are we?" and been answered, "You are in (or,by) the Camels", as the guide told them the name of the district rather than the castle. Translating this misunderstood name into Breton or Welsh might have resulted in 'Y Camellod'.

But there are no stories of a church or chapel near Cadbury Castle or Celliwig where Arthur lies buried. Well did the poet say: 'The world's wonder a grave for Arthur'; nor even do we carry any understanding why there should have been any mystery, any secrecy. South-western Britain was at peace, and the mediaeval idea that Arthur's body was hidden to protect it from desecration by enemies hardly holds water. Might the secrecy not be to convince his *enemies* he was still alive?[22]

Our records of his grave's discovery come mainly from an eccentric, scholarly literary Welshman Giraldus Cambrensis or Gerald of Wales, who was clearly very interested in the event and actually reports it twice. He wrote within a few years of it happening.

Let us begin with a passage from his fragmentary 'Mirror of the Church' surviving in a single manuscript.

'The king [Henry II] had told the abbot on a number of occasions that he had learnt from the historical

The Battle of Camlan and Arthur's Grave | 123

accounts of the Britons and from their bards* that Arthur had been buried in the churchyard there between two pyramids which had been erected subsequently, very deep in the ground for fear that the Saxons, who had striven to occupy the whole island after his death, might ravage the dead body in their evil lust for vengeance.'

Already we run into problems: Henri de Sully became abbot two months *after* Henry's death in 1189. Some mistake seems to have been made unless we believe Henry was in contact with the abbot before he became abbot. Most likely the king had raised the subject with Ranulf de Glanville,† his friend and Chief Justiciar, who, following a terrible fire at the abbey in 1184, was placed in charge to oversee the rebuilding and manage the finances.‡

King Henry had been deeply interested in the wellbeing of the abbey and to that end had allocated considerable funds. These dried up completely after his death. The new abbot was a friend of the new king, Richard I, whose interests lay elsewhere, in the Crusades.

Henri de Sully is himself a cause for concern because his previous abbey, Fécamp in Normandy, had also been devastated by fire: he had raised money for the rebuilding by turning the abbey into a major Norman centre of pilgrimage, in which success Fécamp's holy relics including the blood of Christ and Mary Magdalene's arm bone figured prominently. It would have been a great stroke of

---

* In Gerald's other account, 'an aged British soothsayer'. He also speaks of 'some indications in the Abbey records'.

† Gerald's other account says the king spoke to the monks.

‡ We cannot discount the possibility that there were unsuccessful excavations in the time of Ranulph. Gerald says the site was found 'with immense difficulty... eventually.'

fortune to locate a major tourist attraction at his new abbey.

In 1191, a year and a half after his incumbency began, Henri authorized the digging. Gerald leaves out the important detail supplied by a later historian[*] that the area of excavation had curtains put up around it.

Here, at a depth of 7 ft,[†] the monks dug down to a large stone slab, and, lifting it up, they found affixed to the underside a leaden cross with the inscription: 'Here in the Isle of Avalon lies buried the renowned king Arthur, with Guinevere, his second wife.' The lettering was turned inwards, towards the stone.

Digging down to a total depth of some 16 ft, they reached the object of their search, a hollowed out oak-bole. Here lay bones, and a tress of blonde hair plaited and coiled with consummate skill. A monk jumped into the grave - how he escaped injury is anyone's guess - and grabbed the tress which 'disintegrated into fine powder'.

Gwenhwyfar's body was separate from Arthur's, two thirds of the coffin, towards the top, holding Arthur's bones.[‡] Gerald was shown one of the shinbones by the abbot: it was 'a good three inches' above the knee of the tallest man present when they compared it. The skull was extraordinarily large: between eyebrows and eye-sockets could be fitted the palm of a man's hand! 'Ten or more wounds could clearly be seen, but they had all mended except one. This was larger than the others and it had made an immense gash.' Gerald reckoned this had killed Arthur.

---

[*] Adam of Domerham.

[†] This seems to be the meaning.

[‡] Later, Adam of Domerham says she was interred separately in the grave.

What are we to say about this prodigious corpse? None of the traditions records Arthur as exceptionally large. And the distance between eyebrows and sockets is absurd.*

The detail of the blonde hair is strikingly realistic, and the inscription baffling. No gravestone records *where* one is buried. And yet the curious detail of Gwenhwyfar's being Arthur's second wife is an oddity not easy to comprehend.

It was just about now that the romance was written naming Leonora as Arthur's youthful love; so there might be a link between these two records. Otherwise the inscription could be seen to confirm the earlier relationship of Arthur's.

The curtains are another problem, and 16 ft - onto an oak coffin? - really is a long way to fall.

There's yet another difficulty: a counter-tradition. Ralph of Coggeshall, a reliable contemporary historian, says the coffin (with the leaden cross above it) was found while they were digging a grave for a monk who had ardently desired to be buried precisely there.

Possibly we can name this monk. The 13th century Robert of Gloucester records how in 1183 Saint Egwine was buried in a shrine at Evesham. But his remains were transferred to Glastonbury and buried there subsequently; at which point in his narration Robert mentions the discovery of Arthur, allowing one to speculate that Egwine had been the monk that desired a Glastonbury burial and that the shrine was only intended as a temporary resting-place; but long delay for the transfer had been one consequence of the Glastonbury fire in 1184. Ralph does not mention the pyramids but records the inscription,

---

* Unless the distance is to the bottom of the sockets which have enlarged through collapse of the lower bone structure.

which however does not include Gwenhwyfar.

Clearly, something happened about 1191 at Glastonbury: a hole was dug between two pyramids,[*] and an oak coffin subsequently "emerged" with bones and an inscription. Other details are confused. There is no mention of Arthur's sword presumably given by Abbot Henri to his friend the king, who presented it to Tancred of Sicily in March of the same year.[†]

The inscription can hardly be of the time of Arthur by the style of its lettering, if we are willing to accept the illustration of it prepared by William Camden as accurate, though, like Ralph's version, it does not name Gwenhwyfar. (The cross can be traced down to the 18th century.)

If the lettering is not contemporary one might suspect that a mock-antique inscription was devised for the occasion of the discovery, furthering the claim of Glastonbury to be the legendary Isle of Avalon. Probably the inscription owes a great deal to Geoffrey, even to the use of the word 'inclitus' (renowned).

But, if we discount the inscription (which might after all have been prepared when for some reason Arthur's body had been dug up centuries earlier), there are still the human remains and the oak coffin, and the fact of the depth at which it was buried; perhaps also the stone slab, and even possibly *another* inscription now lost. For Gerald

---

[*] These really existed and are recorded by William of Malmesbury. They were inscribed with the names of the early abbots. But William, as already recorded, knew nothing about Arthur's grave.

[†] The presentation of this sword in early March, 1191 strongly suggests that Adam of Domerham is correct in naming 1190 as the year of the search and discovery.

had examined the inscription closely, and, in both his accounts, he includes Gwenhwyfar: he was not looking at Camden's cross, unless we accuse him of altering the wording, though *his* inscription is quite as problematic. (Dare one suggest that another simpler inscription was adapted by the monks and in more than one version?)

My own feeling would be that something was genuinely discovered but that also *games* were going on. The curtains, and the contradictory evidence relating to the digging, rather suggest this.[*] So does the inscription.

Yes, there is a strong possibility that Arthur and Gwenhwyfar lay buried there.[†] But no, we cannot be certain because of the deeply confusing nature of the information that has come down to us.

---

[*] The main difference between Ralph's version and Giraldus' is that one involves an accidental discovery, the other a search.

[†] Gwenhwyfar's interment would have been the first time Arthur's grave was disturbed, and perhaps the moment to bury Arthur deep. But most probably the precautions taken would have been much later, in the late 6th or the 7th century, when the Saxons were driving westwards.

Chapter 19 - The Historical and Literary Aftermaths

Arthur's death, sad little event that it was, changed nothing. We have seen the coming of the South Saxons and cannot doubt that new Germanic arrivals, especially on the east coast, continued. On the western coast there were a number of Irish expeditions to Britain between 495 and 512, a generation after the Irish settlement that gave its name to the Lleyn peninsula had been wiped out.[*]

However, the Kentish records in the A-S Chronicle fade out, and there is a little indication that some Saxons actually abandoned Britain in the early 6th century.[†] But, for lack of details, conclusions are difficult to draw.

By ingenious use of material in the Saints' lives, John Morris pieced together, in the same period, the story of the campaigning of a Gothic general named Theodoric in South Wales. He speculated that, after the downfall of the Visigothic kingdom in 507 at the hands of the formidable Clovis, the Gothic fleet had lost its Atlantic harbours, and so Theodoric came with all or part of it to offer his services to Britain, and was responsible for the expulsion of the Irish from the South Welsh kingdom of Demetia.[‡]

---

[*] According to my chronology. John Morris believed this was the time of the destruction of the settlement.

[†] The Roman fort of Brittenburg on the Dutch coast was said to have been reoccupied about this time, for instance, which might explain its name. It is now lost under the waves. (William the Chaplain, in 1019, is a late witness to the Saxon exodus.)

[‡] But if the ruling family of Demetia (Dyfed) were of Irish descent (i.e. Vortiporius and his forebears) the Irish were not expelled. So we are told in an Irish work of C.750.

(I place the Irish expulsion a generation earlier and suggest Theodoric defended Wales against renewed Irish incursions.)

One startling arrival at the end of Arthur's lifetime or shortly after is of a man named Cerdic with his son Cynric. These are British names. Evidently, for our source is the A-S Chronicle, they had come at the head of a Saxon force. They carved out the kingdom of Wessex for themselves to the east of Dumnonia, after much fighting with the Britons. One of their victories, assigned by the A-S Chronicle to 508, was against a British king, Natanleod with 5,000 dead from his army. If the king's name is reliable, it may be Pictish.

Here perhaps we can note the shifting alliances and allegiances of the time: a Pict fights at the head of an army of Britons, while their Saxon opponents are led by a Briton. The kingdom of Wessex survived and flourished with its British Dynasty for centuries, so that its greatest king, the 9th century Alfred might still be able to claim that his maternal grandfather was descended from a nephew of Cerdic's.

If we turn again to Gildas' nearly contemporary record of these events belonging to the beginning of his life - I date his book to C.520, others twenty years later - we see that peace prevailed, 'the present calm', 'for our wars may have ceased with foreigners, but not with one another'. On the basis of our separate knowledge of these events, we can see that he is not wholly accurate. From South Wales to Wessex to Sussex, and probably to the north-eastern Saxon kingdoms of Deira and Bernicia (against which Arthur was also probably involved), the British fought with the incoming hordes. One marvels that Gildas makes so light of these activities. Unfortunately we do not know where he was born or lived in his earliest years nor where he dwelt at the time of his writing his book. (It appears probable that in his father's time his family came down from the Scottish kingdom of Strathclyde to Powys in mid-Wales, but we are not sure when though probably very early in his life.) Perhaps it suited his polemic to diminish the struggles with the invaders. For he attempts to tell us that Badon marked an end to nearly all fighting except internal: 'almost the last slaughter ... of the wretches' is how he describes Arthur's great victory. How wary we must be of taking Gildas' words too literally!

In the 540s, a new menace loomed. Travelling from Byzantium, capital of the eastern empire, a deadly plague arrived on British shores. This plague was named the Yellow Pestilence, 'for it caused all persons seized by it to be yellow and bloodless'. It is worth considering that genetically the Britons might have been more vulnerable to the plague than the newcomers, though we have no idea of the casualty rate. Many amongst the Britons may have fled abroad, as St Teilo is said to have done ... 'it seized Maelgwn of Gwynedd and destroyed his country; and so much did the aforementioned devastation rage through the nation that it almost emptied the land of people.' It is certainly about now that the Saxon progress was renewed, especially in respect of the kingdom of Wessex, advancing westward. Following Maelgwn's death in 547, the Britons were routed at Old Sarum by Cerdic's son in 552, and again, at Barbury Castle in 556; in 571 they were defeated at *Biedcanford*, and again in 577 when three British kings were slain at Dyrham, and three important cities, Gloucester, Cirencester and Bath were captured. Though the A-S Chronicle entries favour the Wessex kingdom whose records seem to have survived more completely, there is no mistaking south-western Britain was having a rough time. In the north, Ida united and consolidated the Saxon kingdoms of Deira and Bernicia despite a subsequent scare when his descendants were faced with their kingdom's elimination by a consortium of northern British leaders. But the murder of Urien, king of Rheged by another of the British leaders, out of jealousy over Urien's brilliant generalship destroyed the coalition. Urien was remembered for a three-day blockade of the enemy in the island of Lindisfarne. Amongst the Saxons the important title of Bretwalda was brought back into use; for the kings that followed Aelle had lost it. But it never returned to the South Saxons, the second recipient being recorded by Bede as Ceaulin of the West Saxons, ruling from the mid 6th century.

On the contrary side, we have a bare mention of a resistance leader, Outigirn or Eurdeyrn, very possibly a descendant of Vortigern's, achieving some success against the invaders. In the poems of Taliesin from the mid and late 6th century we catch glimpses of the Saxon leader Fflamddwyn, who was killed by Urien's son. And other indications suggest a strong resistance to the Saxons when the Britons were not fighting amongst themselves.[*] We have seen in Aneirin's poem the disastrous consequences of a courageous British raid into Catterick from the north, probably C.590.

The disparate snippets of historical fact may give us a very limited understanding of what was really happening. But there is no question the British kingdoms fell, in a slow and sad procession. The northern Rheged disappeared almost without a trace of its ever having

---

[*] For instance, the undervalued Book of Llandaff records a grant made by the King of Erging after a (6th century?) victory over the Saxons.

been;* Dumnonia was mostly lost except in its westernmost part (now Cornwall) by C.710;† Elmet (part of modernday Yorkshire) disappeared in the early 7th century: its last king Cerdic - either Cradelmas of the romances or a descendant - had, it seems, incurred the wrath of Edwin of Deira/Bernicia for the killing of a relative. Apart from Cornwall, Wales and Strathclyde survived[23]. But the Britons were truly becoming what their enemies called them - the Welsh, *wealhas* being the foreigners' term for foreigners.

At the end of the 6th century we find the name of Arthur figuring in the genealogies: Arthur map Pedr is a grandson born c.570 of Vortiporius of Demetia one of the five chieftains lambasted by Gildas; while, in the north, Aedan king of the Scots of Dalriada has a son Arthur (Arturius) who dies in 596, battling against the Picts.‡ It is now that we also have our first literary reference to Arthur in Aneirin's striking poem, the Gododdin, where Arthur is clearly seen as a type of fierce warrior. But references to Arthur are scant in our surviving literature for centuries to come, much the most important being the 9th century battle-list of the Historia Brittonum. We cannot doubt that Arthur became a subject of story, though there is no

---

* Celtic was still being spoken in the Cumbrian mountains in the late 16th century amongst the erstwhile Waller-wente (as in former times the Saxons referred to this group of Celts).

† See W.G. Hoskins: Devon (Collins,1954) Pp. 41-2 and K.H. Jackson: Language and History in Early Britain (Edinburgh U.P, 1953) Pp. 205-6 for more detailed Dumnonian chronology.

‡ In the 7th century there are Artuir, son of Bicoir, a Briton and Artur, grandfather of Feradach, a churchman.

evidence that he was the *main* subject that he developed into.

Outside the story-telling tradition, which has left few traces before the 11th century *Culhwch and Olwen* but is galvanized into activity, it would seem, by the publication of Geoffrey's work in the 1130s, we find a few references in the biographies of the Celtic saints. These are important not only for placing Arthur in an historical or pseudo-historical context but for an independent, non-romantic attitude that is sometimes hostile to him.

For instance, in Lifric of Llancarfan's 12th century Life of St Cadoc, Cei and Bedwyr have to restrain the lustful Arthur from the abducted adolescent daughter of Brychan. (This is after a dice match.) But, being dissuaded, Arthur then helps the abductor king, Gundleius of Demetia, against his enemies.*

In the 12th century Life of St Padarn, Arthur is called 'a certain tyrant of that region' who wants to take Padarn's tunic for his own use: he swears, gets into a temper, and kicks things over. In the end he receives Padarn's forgiveness, but even so Padarn refuses to become his mentor.

In the story of Hueil, Arthur is forgiven by Hueil's brother Gildas: grieving and in tears, he is obliged to receive a penance, making amends in any way he can for the rest of his life. Incidentally, Giraldus Cambrensis repeats a story that Gildas' failure to mention Arthur in his work was a consequence of Gildas' anger at Hueil's death.†

---

* The king was father to Cadoc who was said to be instrumental in bringing Illtud into the church, probably in the 460s or 470s.

† Nonsense, of course. But it might be added that Gildas resisted the opportunity to praise the war hero of his youth.

Elsewhere also in Caradoc's life of Gildas, the 'wicked' Melvas snatches Gwenhwyfar away and hides her near Glastonbury. At the end of a year-long search, Arthur comes to fight him 'with the military forces of Cornwall and Devon'. But Gildas comes onto the battlefield to prevent the combat: Gwenhwyfar is restored to Arthur, and the kings give lands to the abbot of Glastonbury before going off to pray and, 'pacified', promising to obey the abbot and not to violate Glastonbury and its environs.

Such stories go some way towards aggrandizing the saints and holy men at the expense of a powerful secular leader. This does not make the stories necessarily untrue except in detail. A measure of hostility might also be suspected from those communities that had once been on the receiving end of such impositions as enforced quartering of soldiers. Roving armies were a source of trouble as well as sometimes of great benefit. But the animosity displayed by the unknown author of St Padarn's Life is a surprise: he virtually reduces Arthur to the status of a local thug!*

One feature of Arthur's life is, actually, his Christianity. At the battle of Castle Guinnion, tentatively placed at Binchester, he is supposed to have borne the image of the Virgin Mary on his shield 'and the *pagans* were put to flight …'; at Mount Badon he is supposed to have borne the image of the cross. A later gloss tells how Arthur went on pilgrimage to Jerusalem, praying before the Lord's Cross for victory over the pagans by means of it, and bringing back an image of the Virgin Mary, the remains of which were still venerated at Wedale in

---

* It is possible to suspect that Arthur was rough and overbearing in his dealings with the church. Baring-Gould's opinion of him is quite scathing.

Lothian. (Possibly Stow on the Scottish borders, where there is a church dedicated to St Mary, is intended.)

This story, while perhaps inspired by the Christian detail in the battle of Castle Guinnion to which it is attached, may show a memory of a legend genuinely once connected with Wedale, and placing Arthur in a Christian light. We must not forget that his first cousin was one of the earliest of the Celtic Saints, studying, it would seem, under bishop Germanus. And we cannot rule out the possibility that Arthur was another pupil of Germanus'.

Giraldus Cambrensis records, at the end of the 12th century, that Arthur was a great patron of Glastonbury Abbey and was 'highly praised in their records'. He loved the Church (dedicated to the Virgin Mary) more than any other place of worship. Giraldus continues: 'When he went out to fight, he had a full-length portrait of the Blessed Virgin painted on … his shield, so that in the heat of battle he could always gaze upon Her; and whenever he was about to make contact with the enemy he would kiss Her feet with great devoutness.'

There is nothing impossible in all this, but Giraldus fails to quote from the Abbey records, and now was the time of the 'discovery' of Arthur's grave. At least, he does not follow the Historia Brittonum or Annales Cambriae in placing the image on Arthur's shoulders. We must allow the possibility that there is a genuine foundation for what he says, though a Glastonbury tradition (which this surely is) must be sadly suspect. If the earlier records *single out* the battles of Castle Guinnion and Mount Badon - and some think there is a certain ancient confusion between the two in their Christian detail - it is certainly not very likely Arthur had Christian shield images for his other battles.

Perhaps, after all, Castle Guinnion was the only battle[*] in which Christian imagery was employed. And yet that is enough to tell us that Arthur was capable of fighting in the name of Christianity and was himself Christian. It is regrettable how difficult it remains to isolate the characteristics of the Britons' remarkable leader. A man of faith perhaps, this educated aristocrat, grandson of a king and great grandson of the legendary Cunedda, giving him many distinguished cousins from the saintly Illtud to the powerful Maelgwn, we see as a hugely successful general and strategist but little else.

The Camlan episode seems to have been a somewhat silly event, a small thing blown out of all proportion. It might be attributable to his temper or folly, but he was an old man and is hardly to be judged on this. It is easy to suppose him charismatic and effortlessly engaging the loyalty of his followers, a dynamic force like the no less remarkable Charles XII of Sweden. His involvement with Cei and Bedwyr was enduring, though Cei was absent from Camlan, perhaps dead or too old: legend speaks of an enmity that grew between them.

A triad (12) speaks of Arthur as one of the three frivolous bards, perhaps with reference to his amateur status. There are several englynion or verses assigned to him of a more or less satirical nature. In *Culhwch and Olwen*, it is one of these that gives lasting offence to Cei. For example, these are the words he spoke to a certain Cribwr of Glamorgan whose sisters he had killed:

> Cribwr, take these your combs
> And cease your churlish anger.

---

[*] The story being subsequently transferred to the more famous battle.

If I obtain a chance- surely
What they have had, you shall have too.

One might also note ironically his fondness for women. In addition to Leonora and Gwenhwyfar, his name is linked with several others: Drudwas, son of Tryffin is named in an ancient list as one of the three golden-tongued knights of Arthur's court along with Gwalchmei; and again in a triad with Gwalchmei and also Cei, as an owner of 'bestowed horses'.

A prominent member of Arthur's following, then, he is said to have had a sister, Erdudfyl, who was Arthur's mistress. Her father's name, derived from the Latin *tribunus*, suggests a Roman background. One folktale fantasy recorded in the early 17th century includes her, but another (17th century) version does not: she saves Arthur's life, but, unwittingly, at the expense of her brother's.

Another triad (57) names three others: Indeg, daughter of Garwy the Tall; Garwen daughter of Henin the Old; and Gwyl, daughter of Gendawd. Of these, Indeg was renowned for her beauty, and herself daughter of a famous lover while Garwen appears to have survived, like Tegau, mistress of Caradawc Vreichvras, as a symbol of constancy and fidelity. An old stanza indicates she was buried on the sea-shore; this was probably near Llandudno. Both Tegau and Garwen are named in a 13th century English lyric, *Annot and Johon*: 'Trewe ase Tegeu in tour, ase Wyrwein in wede'. This might give us grounds for supposing that Garwen (Wyrwein) was Arthur's mistress at the time of Camlan and wore mourning attire (wede) for the rest of her life in faithfulness to his memory.*

While it is beyond the scope of this little work to trace the development of the Arthurian story, we need not hesitate to believe in a vibrant oral tradition over the early centuries, especially amongst the Welsh and Bretons. The storytellers are seldom known to us by name, but one Bledhericus referred to by Giraldus may survive as Blaise, Merlin's master in the romances.

The Norman conquest of 1066 was a huge factor in the transmission of the stories. Many Bretons fought beside William the Conqueror and were given land in Britain. We have also seen in the conquest of Sicily that there must have been Breton storytellers in the Norman entourage. As well as several Sicily-based stories of Arthur, we have still earlier the first appearance of Arthur in art, in the archivolt over a door of Modena Cathedral on the Italian mainland dated to C.1106. (In this sculpture Arthur and his knights attack a castle.)

Geoffrey's work of 1136 fanned flames of enthusiasm, perhaps a source of ironic humour to the Norman overlords observing, however gradually, the Englishmen's increasing interest in their own people's

---

* I do not think Garwen's name (= fair leg) any more than Gwyl's (= modest) should count against their reality. Garwen's looks like a nickname. Gruffudd ap Maredudd speaks of '... the care of Arthur of the highlands of Britain for the daughter of Garwy Hir.' The 'highlands of Britain' give one food for thought: is the poet thinking of another Arthur or does he know something we do not?

great adversary of long ago.* Where are the stories of Hereward the Wake, the Normans' great English adversary, now?† In Britain and across the Continent, Arthur became the great vogue subject, reflecting mediaeval ideals of chivalry, constancy and faith. One special new feature was the Holy Grail, the scarcely attainable Christian(?) treasure, which has fascinated and bewildered readers to the present day.

But the Arthur of history was being lost. A post-Roman British general, whom no contemporary wrote about, is hardly to be considered of overwhelming significance, and, while he controlled the invading peoples, he did not succeed in expelling them.‡ Within two centuries of his death, even most of his beloved Dumnonia was in their hands. How much more attractive was Geoffrey's all-conquering emperor!

William Caxton knew of a wax seal encased in beryl that could be seen at the shrine of Edward the Confessor at Westminster when he published Malory's work in the 1480s. It bore the Latin words translatable as 'Arthur,

---

* In the mid-12th century, Ailred abbot of Rievaulx recalled how a novice monk told him how he would cry over tales of Arthur. Walter Daniel believed these stories derived from Breton conteurs visiting Yorkshire. We can imagine the English caught in a kind of cultural crossfire between the overlord Celts i.e. Bretons, conquerors with William at Hastings, and the despised or hostile Celts i.e. Welsh.

† Once popular in literature and ballad, most material relating to him has been long lost.

‡ It may be argued that by slowing down the Saxon advance he made the transition to Saxon rule gentler but I remain convinced that we retain, despite our chronicles, no concept of how this period was awash with blood.

emperor of Britain, France, Germany and Denmark, patrician'.

This may have survived till at least 1531 when the Duke of Norfolk, trying to emphasize England's status as an empire, produced the inscription for the imperial ambassador's inspection. But the ambassador Eustace Chapuys responded with irony, not attempting to deny that this might once have been true, but pointing out that 'as all things in this world were so subject to change' how fatuously irrelevant it was, though he expressed himself more gently.

Chapuys' rather disrespectful reply probably reflected not only political reality but a growing realization that the mediaeval Arthur, from Geoffrey onwards, was a storybook character and scarcely in the realms of historical truth.

From Chapuys' time forward, the Arthur of history and literature has been somewhat in eclipse. And latterly it is the scholars of these subjects who have taken most interest with a vast swarm of amateur enthusiasts tagging along behind.

As late as the early 19th century, there were still Welshmen remembering Arthur's name in proverbs: 'Arthur was not, but whilst he was,' (spoken of a great family reduced to indigence), and: 'King Arthur did not violate the refuge of a woman,' (intimating that he left her the free use of her tongue).[*]

Such lingering traces some 1300 years after his death are testimony to the extraordinary resilience of the interest in an heroic soldier from so distant a time. And yet, at the

---

[*] Letters written during a Tour through South Wales. Rev J Evans. 1804. There is no other record of Arthur as victim of Gwenhwyfar's verbal abuse.

end of this little work, filled with my numerous attempts to present possibilities and likelihoods about my subject, there is one fact that it is pointless to deny: *certain* proofs of the reality of Arthur remain lacking.*[24] Nor is there much reason to suppose this state of affairs will ever alter.

Arthur exists in an historical limbo like a word on the tip of one's tongue. I live on a hillside at the top of which Arthur stood and played quoits in the form of boulders with the devil.† The "quoits" fell between them at the magnificent pile of rocks over there, 2 miles off to the east, which was also one of the locations for an Arthurian film in the 1950s. Out of sight a half mile to the north stood (I believe) Arthur's Throne or Chair, a granite enclosure (probably a hide) pulled down less than a century ago in the course of field clearance.‡ If I climb to the top of the hill I can stare across towards the ruined remains of what was once known as Arthur's Oven, formerly a smelting house for tin.§ And indeed some

---

* There was great excitement in 1998 at the Tintagel discovery of a 6th century inscription naming one *Arth*nou, who might be a relative of Arthur's. See Supplementary Note 24. I would stress that those who seek to undermine the Historia Brittonum battle-list imply a dishonesty in the compiler *of which there is no other indication*.

† The devil was in the region of Lustleigh. Perhaps Lustleigh Cleave. However Cecil Torr who records this knew that the devil dwelt in Yarner Wood, from which he once had to escape at dusk in panic flight. Arthur stood on Hameldown Ridge, and the pile created was Haytor Rocks.

‡ Kings Head: the name is derived from King's Seat.

§ King's Oven is on the high ground behind the Warren House Inn. We may note Chaw Gully on the other side of the road. Once a home of choughs, it fits tidily into the legend that Arthur survived as a chough or raven.

monks were told over nine centuries ago that this part of Devon, anciently in mid-Dumnonia, was 'Arthur's own land'. Arthur lives on, a will o' the wisp, a phantom, like his sister Morgana. His elusiveness has its own charm, presents its own challenge. He is assured of a peculiar immortality as each succeeding generation goes in search of him, less important for what he was than for what we make of him. Rex quondam rexque futurus: The 'King' That Was and Will Be has never really gone away.

ENVOI

One 'characteristic' we assign inevitably to Arthur is his ubiquitousness: from the south-west peninsula to Wales, from Anglesey and the Isle of Man to Yorkshire and Northumberland, and northward into Scotland, a variety of legends concerned primarily with his combating giants and monsters, or waiting in secret till the time of his return,[*] spill across Britain, and occasionally abroad. Sometimes we may suspect his name has replaced a still older one in the story. Plutarch's tale of Kronos, father of Zeus, kept imprisoned on an island off Britain, surrounded by gods and attendants, for instance, closely parallels Arthur underground or in a cavern, surrounded by his knights, as we find several times over.[†] In the following ballad from Brittany preserved by La Villemarqué we see Arthur at the head of his army - led by cavalry on grey steeds, be it noted - ascending a mountain which La Villemarqué takes to be part of the Breton mountain range, the Black Mountains. But it might equally well be a mountain in Britain, Agned, perhaps, or Badon. It was sung by Breton soldiers marching, to war, and the man who recited it to La Villemarqué, an old ex-Chouan[‡]

---

[*] The Northern stories about Arthur - especially his sleeping till the right time - seem to further belief of his extensive Northern battles. In particular, we must remember the Saxons were south *and* north. (The Scottish Dumfries is the fortress of the Frisians.)

[†] The closest parallel I have found to Plutarch's story is of a giant under Castle Rushen on the Isle of Man, which island I take to be the original site of the story.

[‡] One of those who, in the Revolution, fought as a Royalist in the Vendée. They were hideously treated by the likes of Carrier.

of Leuhan had often sung it, so he said, while on the march in the last wars of the West, the wars of Napoleon.

The March of Arthur

"Lets's be going, going to the battle! Go parent - go,
    brother - go, son - go, father - go, go, all, go then,
    men of spirit!

The warrior's son told his father in
    the morning: "Horsemen on the
                    mountain top!
Horsemen passing mounted on grey
    coursers snorting with the cold!
Ranged in ranks six by six; ranged
    in ranks three by three; a thousand
    lances glittering in the sun.
Ranged in ranks two by two, following
    The standards swaying in the
                    Wind of Death.
Nine lengths of a sling's cast from
    their head to their tail.
It's the army of Arthur, I'm certain:
Arthur marches at their head
    to the heights of the mountain."

"If it's Arthur, quickly to our
    bows and our ready arrows.
And onward after them, and
    may our darts not be idle!"
Before he finished speaking the
    warcry echoed from one side
    of the mountains to the other:
"A heart for an eye! A head for

an arm! And death for a wound,
in the valley as much as on the
mountain! And father for mother,
and mother for daughter!
A stallion for a mare, and a
mule for an ass! A general for
a trooper, and adult for a child!

Blood for tears, and flames for
sweat!
And three for one (as must
be done) in the valley as
much as on the mountain,
- day and night if one can -
till the valleys flow with
streams of blood!
[If we fall stricken in the
combat, we shall be baptized
with our own blood and die
with joyous hearts.
If we die as Christians and Bretons should,
never shall we die too soon!"][*]

---

[*] The bracketed verses are considered a later addition.

APPENDICES

Appendix 1 - A Note on the Author's Speculative Method

The history of this obscure period comes from fragmentary literary sources supplemented by modern archaeology. It is a kind of jigsaw with many of the pieces forever missing. It is therefore *unusually legitimate* to try to build up the limited picture by attempting to tease out extra information from such sources as we possess, although we at once enter the realms of probable rather than exact history - if history can ever be said to be exact!

In Chapter One, to take an extreme example, I have silently speculated in order to try to add to the historical picture. For instance, the scene of the murders was an abbey or monastery in the Westcountry i.e. Dumnonia. (And a purist might attempt to argue that even Dumnonia is unproven.) But we know of very few abbeys or monasteries in Dumnonia in this period, and the one of greatest significance and status was surely Glastonbury (from its primitive foundation and religious communities that grew up around it.); so that Glastonbury Abbey becomes an acceptable speculation.[*]

No armed retainers are mentioned nor are the abbot's robes (which are noted) mentioned as a disguise. But again it seems not unlikely.

The two young aristocrats I hypothesize as rightful heirs to the throne. For at once we have a simple

---

[*] Its antiquity is exemplified by the Old Church, built of wattle, and modernized probably in the late 5th century with wooden planks and lead by Paulinus, most likely St David's mentor, also said to have been a disciple of Germanus. The abbey was hugely venerated after C.500; Gildas is said to have been 'charmed by the sanctity of the place'.

explanation for the gruesome event: Constantine if he was younger brother to the recently deceased king would have to eliminate the king's male children before being able to claim his own right to the succession.* I suggest the young men were under-age, perhaps in their late teens, and Constantine their uncle had earlier that year been appointed regent of Dumnonia during their minority, which was why he had to make a formal oath, as Gildas tells us, to do no harm to his people. (But he had other plans than the regency!)

Again, I would propose: isn't it possible that Gildas had received knowledge directly from their mother? I suggest this because he makes no description of her feelings. It would be so much more normal to say the murders took place in front of the *distraught* mother. But Gildas says nothing about her, perhaps to deflect Constantine's attention away from her as Gildas' source of knowledge.

In addition, when Gildas describes, in somewhat ridiculous terms, their warrior prowess, isn't this a nod towards the contents of the letter he received? He is repeating a mother's loving and exaggerated description of what her darlings were capable of - an ingenious way of conveying something of her feelings, and showing her his respect and sympathy.

One might also be led to conclude that Gildas was personally known to her from having visited or lived in the Westcountry.

The arguments for the friendship between Cadwy and Arthur are, as so often, somewhat circumstantial. From an old poem, it appears that Arthur fought beside Cadwy's

---

* They might of course be *another* older brother's sons.

A Note on the Author's Speculative Method

father at the battle of Llongborth. The father died that day and Cadwy became the new king of Dumnonia, if we assume his father was king at the time. Cadwy was famous in story, according to the 9th century Wrdisten, implying a longish life after the battle. For the last 20 years or so of Arthur's life Arthur may well have been living in eastern Dumnonia at Cadbury Castle, protecting the eastern and northern borders of the kingdom. He was probably positioned near the residence of Cadwy, whose main church, at Glastonbury, was 11 miles from the Castle. In a story, in the 12th (?) century Life of Carantoc, Arthur and Cadwy (Cato) are found reigning together in (eastern ?) Dumnonia, at Dindraithou, perhaps Dunster. This co-reign may be an attempt to square "King" Arthur's presence with a king already known to have existed there. To my mind, these disparate pieces of data amount to a fair likelihood of a friendship between the two of them at the end of Arthur's life. (Geoffrey, naturally enough, reverses their positions and makes Cador Duke of Cornwall a loyal supporter of Arthur's).*

---

* There may be some deliberate confusion here by Geoffrey with the Cador who was deposed as earl of Cornwall at the time of the Norman Conquest. In 1104 Cador's grand-daughter married Henry I's son, Reginald, who then claimed the earldom of Cornwall.

Appendix 2 - Dating Arthur's Birth

We have seen that Arthur's first cousin Illtud is said to have studied under Germanus undoubtedly near the end of Germanus' life, as perhaps did Arthur. Germanus died most probably in 444 or 448, dating Illtud's birth to the 430s, if the story is true.

Illtud is said to have visited Arthur on the way to take up his position as Magister Militum (Troop Commander) at the court of King Poulentus in Wales. I suggest that this visit really took place, and that Arthur's younger cousin was in attendance on a well-established older relative of the same generation. I have given reasons why Arthur may have been involved at the beginning of his career in a successful battle with Chlodio king of the Franks, most probably in the 440s. This battle was probably a little later than Vicus Helena dated to C.440. If this is so, Arthur must have been born no later than the 420s, and this is hardly surprising if he had won the friendship of so powerful a figure as Aegidius by the 460s.

Lastly I have given reasons for placing Badon in 479, and Camlan therefore - following the Annales Cambriae time interval - close to 500. This really would preclude Arthur's birth before 420, for there are few warriors that ever went out to battle in their 80s. The remarkable Byzantine general Liberius, aged about 85 was one exception in the following century, and he was probably exceeded by his fellow-commander, Narses.

Appendix 3 - The Last Legions in Britain

Our early literary information on the final visits of Roman armies to these shores is almost entirely derived from Gildas. In Chapters 15-19 of his work, he tells us how Britain sent envoys with a letter to Rome and that they were rewarded for their pains with the quick dispatch of a legion that was very successful in its British campaign.

After their return, the defeated enemies reappeared as before 'spreading destruction everywhere'. A second embassy was sent, and Gildas knew the tradition that they put on a tragical histrionic display, tearing their clothes and covering their heads in dust. (This last detail was known to the compiler of the Historia Brittonum who also added that they brought great gifts for 'the consuls' i.e. at Rome, not Ravenna) Another hugely successful British campaign followed. It may be true, as in Gildas' version, that the Romans left behind manuals for weapon training or prototype weapons when they departed.

But when was it? Gildas' only clue is that some period had passed after Maximus' execution (in 388) before the first of the visiting legions. He also seems to refer to the Hallelujah victory in 429 as postdating the last legion. But Gildas is working from traditional knowledge, and his historical framework is vague and not really to be considered reliable. What we do know of is the campaigning in the North by Stilicho in the 390s, which might connect us with the first of Gildas' legions. But so many events followed in the period 407-11, especially Constantine's rebellion, when Britain seems to have had far more than a skeletal Roman command that it is tempting to look for both legions in a later period. And curiously there are three late mediaeval historians who concur in this view. Blondus, Sabellicus and Hector Boece are scarcely names to set the historiographic world alight. And Boece, a Scotsman, may be safely discounted as leaning on one of the earlier authorities. But the circumstantial accounts of the other two surely deserve a little consideration[25].

Sabellicus tells us how the Picts and Scots, under the pretext of a treaty, tried to claim Britain for themselves[*] ... 'Britain was then helpless. Aetius fearful of that [claim] and worn out by the pleadings of those who were still loyal, sent one legion from Gaul into the island ...and the state of the island became much more pacified than for a long time previously.'

But the legion had to be recalled, for the Burgundians were 'intent on new disturbances' - Sabellicus says they were invading Gaul. 'Leaving one legion to defend the people of Orleans and Paris, and a second to defend the Iberian Tarragonians, he [Aetius] advanced with the remaining strength of his forces.'

New troubles followed in Britain. "When this was made known to Valentinian, he ordered that the legion which Aetius had designated to defend the people of Sens, Orleans and Paris be transported into the British provinces under Gallio of Ravenna..."

Is this then the last legion? An earlier historian, the 12th century Sigebert of Gembloux, tells us: 'On the Britons' promising once more their submission to Roman authority Honorius sent help; and [at that time] the Spanish were struggling in a war with the Vandals; but it [Honorius' help] had no effect' - perhaps suggesting that temporary success could not solve the Britons' troubles. The Vandal war in Spain dates this help to 422, just before

---

[*] foederis praetextu ... insulam vendicare.

Honorius' death.[26]

So a consistent picture could emerge - of a legion sent by Aetius (whether or not under the emperor Honorius' orders) C.422 - and of its recall by Aetius because of problems with the Burgundians whom Aetius marched against - Gaul, not Spain being his main sphere of authority.

Then, after Honorius' death, probably within 2 years of the return of the first legion, the Parisian legion was sent under the instructions of the imperial authorities,[*] and with a general chosen from the imperial Ravenna circle. I cannot see anything unreasonable about this. Aetius' career is sufficiently obscure at this point to allow the possibility of such events. But we really have no clue to the authorities Blondus and Sabellicus were employing. At any rate they provide the only clear and definite statements of the last legions, for what that is worth[†].

---

[*] Valentinian was a boy of 6 at his accession. His mother Placidia would probably have had the main hand in such a decision. The 14th century Byzantine Nicephorus (Book XIV cap. 56 of his Ecclesiastical History) tells us how, through Valentinian's negligence and silliness, he soon lost Britain, Spain and Gaul. The much earlier Theophanes dates the same to 439. A work of the 440s records Britain's loss in 410 'forever'.

[†] I have mentioned also Sigebert's remark, to which might be added a quotation of Paulus Diaconus. Sigebert's Chronicle ends in 1112. All these sources are to be found in the pages of Archbishop Ussher's Britannicarum Ecclesiarum Antiquitates (1687) Pp. 313 ff. Sigebert is not perhaps the most reliable historian but may have used lost sources. I regret I can say nothing of the calibre of Sabellicus, but Blondus, the secretary of several popes, wrote what was considered, in his own time, a model history.

Appendix 4 - Hengest and Hnaef

It is quite possible we know a small piece of Hengest's background history. A fragment of nearly 50 lines of an Old English poem was put into print in 1705 by the scholar George Hickes. He had found it in Lambeth Palace Library, but the original does not survive. Oddly enough, a portion of narrative that is related to the story in the fragment is also found in the Old English epic Beowulf, but the complete story still eludes us.

It would seem that a party of Danes under the leadership of Hnaef visited the king of the Frisians at a place called Finnsburh. A fight started: Hnaef's men were attacked by night. Both the king's son and Hnaef were killed before the king came to terms with the Danes' new leader, Hengest - terms that included Hengest's killing of his own lord; and the Danes stayed for the winter. In the spring, however, they turned on the Frisians, killing their king and returning home with his wife, quite probably Hnaef's sister.

These events could easily have led to Hengest's banishment, and his son's too if he had been present. We may have the good fortune to be witnessing the very circumstances leading to their arrival in Britain.

Appendix 5 - The Letter to Aetius

Unexpected confirmation for the dating of the British letter to exactly 446 is to be found in another 446 document. (It has been possible to believe that the letter's reference to Aetius' 3rd consulship in 446 may be retrospective from any time up to his death in 454).

Aetius' panegyrist, the Spaniard, Flavius Merobaudes produced a rambling poem to celebrate his achievements and consulate. In one section (not relating to Britain) we find curious parallels: a people is threatened with loss of their land, and with being driven into the sea.

'The sea drives us back' (Gildas) is not dissimilar to 'we are cast down by the waves'; 'between these [ordeals] appear two kinds of death' (Gildas) is much like 'perish by one of two fates'.

I believe the letter to Aetius is being paraphrased, its tragic content having made a deep impression on Merobaudes and others; and that this paraphrase was meant to stir Aetius' feelings when he heard it. From the next lines of Merobaudes, perhaps we can reconstruct another portion of the letter: *'But do not let us endure these things unavenged, ...we implore you to grant that our complaints meet with the due outcome.'*

The Latin runs:
1. Repellit nos mare. (Gildas)
   Depellim<ur undis. (Merobaudes)
2. Inter haec oriuntur duo genera funerum. (Gildas)
   Alterna sub sorte perit. (Merobaudes)

And Merobaudes' continuation:
Nec inulta<feremus / haec tamen: et nostris aderit

sors ius<ta querelis.*

The full Latin text of Merobaudes runs: [A goddess speaks]
... Sic cuncta
      mei revere<ntia regni
Alterna sub sorte perit:
      depellim<ur undis
Nec terris regnare licet.
      Nec inulta <feremus
Haec tamen et nostris
      aderit sors ius<ta querelis.†

---

* Literally: Yet we shall not endure these things unavenged; and our complaints will meet with the due outcome.

† I cannot follow those who believe that 'three times consul' is a parenthetical remark inserted by Gildas. Gildas' expression for Aetius, 'powerful Roman' (literally 'man of Roman power') pretty clearly indicates that Gildas knew nothing about him; from which we are probably to infer Gildas' massive ignorance of 5th century historical sources. It may be added that the careful Gildas would have placed the description 'three times consul' *before* the quoted passages if it had been his own. Gildas' ignorance suggests also that he had not travelled on the Continent.

Appendix 6 - Arthur in Carlisle

Though the romances often place Arthur in the north, especially linking him with his Court at Carlisle, the evidence for Arthur's presence in Carlisle is often overlooked.*

In the reign of Henry II a charter was confirmed that had been originally made in his father Henry I's time. The charter stated that Ranulf son of Walter granted land around Arthur's *burh* in Carlisle, next to the house of the [Augustinian] canons - a *burh* being a fortified manor or mansion. This dates the original reference to no later than 1135, and before Geoffrey.

In 1610, John Denton of Cardew, a local historian, wrote: 'Waldeive, son of Gospatrick, earl of Dunbar gave to the priory [of Carlisle]... a mansion near St Cuthbert's church where *at that time* stood an ancient building called Arthur's chamber taken to be part of the mansion house of King Arthur ...' Waldeive's gift of the house near the church is officially recorded, and of the 12th century.

And here the matter rests at present. Marjorie Howling suggests that Denton's reference to Arthur's chamber as part of King Arthur's mansion house may derive directly from an authority he names and uses - 'the monk who wrote the history of Arthur'.

From a broader point of view, we see how Carlisle, so proximate to Hadrian's Wall, south of which was British territory, was a perfect vantage-point for any northern campaign - whether directly against Picts and Scots to the north or against the new Saxon settlements in Deira and

---

* The Welsh tradition knew of another northern site associated with Arthur - Pen(ryn) Rionyt. But we don't know where it was.

Bernicia to the east or to protect Arthur's nephew's kingdom, Galloway, a handful of miles north-west from sundry foes, Saxons and Picts, and Scots but perhaps from enemies within the British kingdom of Strathclyde as well.

The king of Strathclyde, Coroticus, and his soldiers were recipients of an angry letter from St Patrick C.450 for Coroticus' enslaving Christianized Irishmen. St Patrick calls him a tyrant. Legend says that Coroticus mocked at these 'salutary warnings' and was turned into a fox.

Carlisle may have been the administrative centre, the capital so to speak, of the British kingdom, Rheged. Though not extensively excavated, it contains evidence *inter alia* of a 5th century 'large hall-like building'.

Appendix 7 - The Date of the Battle of Mount Badon

Gildas' convoluted text runs as follows: 'From that time [when Ambrosius took the leadership and had a victory] sometimes our countrymen sometimes the enemy were successful ... up to the year of the siege of Mount Badon, almost the last and one of the greatest slaughters of the wretches ... which was the 44th year (as I know) that began, one month already having passed, which is also my birth-year.'

Gildas was born in the year of the battle and knows precisely, down to the month, when the battle occurred. (I have already suggested he places it in the second month, though 'the first' might have been more expected than 'one'.)

But the significant question is whether we trace back the 44 years from the writing of Gildas' book or forward from Ambrosius. In other words, is Gildas trying to say, as I believe: 44 years and the second month since the beginning of the war; or, 44 years and one month ago?

In defence of my position, I would suggest that, without Gildas' having a date for the beginning of the war, he knew it as the 44 years' War (like the 7 years' War or the 30 years' War). I would also point out that Bede believed as I do, though he chose a slightly different starting-point. Furthermore, is there any point in Gildas' telling us that the event was 44 years before, if he does not tell us the year of writing? His work was more than an ephemeral tract and intended to endure.

But the only certainty is that Badon was the year of Gildas' birth. This is something. Gildas wrote his book before 547 when Maelgwn died, and before the plague which caused Maelgwn's death and which had been prevalent for several years already: this would surely have figured as a judgement of God in Gildas' book, and likewise some exceptionally harsh winters in the 530s.

I have placed Gildas' book at C.520, this being a relatively early point in his career: he died half a century later. There are no strong or decisive arguments. I suggest the fiery courage of this educated man - he studied under Illtud as did Maelgwn - who can probably quote the Bible at will, might place Gildas in his 30s or 40s. He says he has delayed writing already for more than a decade, naming his inexperience as a main reason.

By another tack, let us take as our starting point the question directed at Maelgwn of Gwynedd, 'dragon of the island' and one of the five leaders vituperated by Gildas for their ungodly ways: 'Did you not, in the first years of your youth, use sword and spear and flame in the cruel despatch of the king your uncle and his bravest soldiers, as it were, whose features in battle array much resembled those of young lions?

This vivid quotation ranks amongst Gildas' most informative utterances: it appears to tell us that many years before the writing of his book, Gildas had seen some of those troops employed by Ewein Danwyn to defend himself against his young nephew.* This war followed the death of Cadwallawn Llawhir, the father of Maelgwn, when Maelgwn sought to increase his father's kingdom by seizing his uncle's. This war took place when, or before, Ambrosius' grandson was on his throne whose father we

---

* 'In battle array' is, literally, *in line of battle*. I do not think Gildas watched them fighting nor borrowed the description of their features from some eyewitness: he saw them on the way to the battlefield.

know was not long-lived. And tracking back from Maelgwn's death in 547 when he had evidently became a by-word for longevity, we can see it most likely belongs to the 490s, and at the latest the 500s. The brothers Ewein and Cadwallawn numbered amongst their first cousins Cei's father and Arthur's mother, whom, through other descents from Cunedda, I believe to have been somewhat older than the royal brothers. This strongly suggests to me that Gildas' birth, and Badon, took place no later than the 480s, though it is of course conceivable that Gildas might have been a very tiny boy when Ewein's troops passed by and so much impressed him.

Appendix 8 - (South) Cadbury Castle

It is reasonable to identify Arthur's western Dumnonian fortress, Celli Wig with a real place named Kellewik. We know of this place only because a certain Thomas de Kellewik was murdered at Gulval, just north-east of Penzance in the far west of Cornwall, at the beginning of the 14th century. Kellewik was probably close by. The neighbouring hill-fort of Castle-an-Dinas has been proposed, while Kelly Rounds (Killibury Castle) is a still more obvious choice; it is near Wadebridge some way to the north, but also much nearer Tintagel. But doubts even as to the meaning of Celli Wig deny us all certainty.

Celli Wig may have fallen victim to the great raid of 452:[*] 'when Celli was lost, there was fury,' says an old poem with Arthurian content. But in happier times perhaps Illtud visited; this may also have been the setting for meetings between Gwenhwyfar and Medraut, who appears to have been based in Cornwall.

Arthur's eastern Dumnonian residence is a different story. From at least the Tudor antiquarian Leland's time, the hillfort at South Cadbury in Somerset was equated with the Camelot of the romances. Here Arthur 'much resortid'. Archaeology under Leslie Alcock - from 1966 to 1970 - demonstrated that, after a break, the site was newly

---

[*] But more probably it was sacked via a sea raid or seized in the course of internal fighting. Cornish tradition had many stories of Arthur fighting enemies in this far Western vicinity. In the battle of Vellan-Druchar Arthur and nine Kings destroyed a Danish naval force much as Clovis' grandson did to Hygelac in the early 6th century. Lady Charlotte Guest indicated a story that Medraut seized it, but her context was the romance tale of Medraut's usurpation. Triad 54 (see Cap.17) might suggest something similar.

occupied in the late 5th century; and the occupation continued through the 6th, dying out in the 7th century.

There had been considerable strengthening of the innermost of several ramparts covering the whole three quarters of a mile of its length. There was extensive use of timber, and reuse of Roman masonry.

A large quantity of post-holes were also discovered testifying to a large building over 60 feet long, possibly a great hall.

This originally Iron Age fortress stands to a height of over 500 feet. Its steep sides contain an area of some 18 acres and it may have needed the best part of 1,000 men to man its defences. A timber gate-tower stood at the south-western entrance: possibly based on a Roman model, it was repaired in the period after Maelgwn's death when the Saxons were sweeping into the west.

None of this, nor pottery fragments and other small-scale finds, proves the fort to have belonged to Arthur. But it did belong to an important late 5th century soldier or civilian with many men under his command.

We may add the tradition recorded by Elis Gruffudd that Arthur may lie buried there;[*] and even at the end of the 19th century an old native of the place greeted an antiquarian with these words: 'Have you come to take the king out?'

Lastly, there is Leland's story of the finding of a silver horse-shoe, which he connects with the ghostly troop of Arthur and his knights seen riding around the hill in the moonlight.[†] Fifty years after Leland's time, Camden

---

[*] If he is not referring to Glastonbury Tor.

[†] I will note here that a Dartmoor tor (in a strongly defensive position) has been the site of a haunting by Roman soldiers seen encamped there at night. Lately a Roman coin of the Emperor Hadrian's was discovered at this very

reported that 'the local people call it Arthur's Palace.*'

---

tor.

* A second large and important site at Congresbury nearby was also occupied in the same period. It has been called 'high-status' but its use remains uncertain, nor are there traditions relating to it.

Appendix 9 - A Westcountry visitor from Constantinople

Since Arthur may have been lord of lands in Devon, and on Dartmoor specifically (see last paragraph of the final chapter) I note here the delightful tale incorporated into a Byzantine sermon and rediscovered by Baring-Gould. This is only the second evidence of Westcountry tinning in the post-Roman period so far found: baldly stated, it is of a Constantinople merchant Theodorus fallen on hard times who borrows money from a Jew Abram, before embarking on a long and successful sea journey culminating in his ship's arrival in a bay off the Cornish coast. Here on landing he buys tin and lead very cheaply and re-embarks. His subsequent adventures and the miraculous way he sends advance payment to his usurer friend lead to his friend's conversion to Christianity.

Abram appears to have been a known historical figure, and we can hesitantly date the story to C. 540. It was probably written up for the sermon in the 10th century.[*]

From almost the same date, a half-century after Arthur's death when Constantine might have consolidated his position on the throne of Dumnonia, come the plaintive words of another inhabitant of Constantinople, the poet and scholar Agathias Scholasticus of Myrina, harking back to a distant past:

---

[*] For the full story, see Historic Oddities and Strange Events (1901). Pp. 103-121. The Greek text is found in Combefisius - Auctuarium Novum, pars post. Col 664. This summary does no justice to the charm of the original.

And you, western maidservant, beyond Cadiz
And beside the Spanish Strait and Oceanic Thule,
Breathe easily, and of successive tyrants
Counting the heads buried in your dust,
Receive your beloved Rome with confident hands.*

But perhaps this view, however anachronistic, was shared by the person responsible for the Welsh grave inscription datable by the words 'In the time of the consul Justinus' to 540!

---

* From Agathias' Proem to the Greek Anthology. The maidservant is Britain, and Thule, to the north, Greenland perhaps.

Appendix 10 - Lancelot

One of the principal knights of Arthur springs into life in the late 12th century in the pages of Chrétien de Troyes and likewise of Marie de France, by whom however he is called Launval. He is named as a king's son from a foreign land by Marie, who claims her lay (as customarily) as a Breton tale.

In subsequent writings, he is called the son of King Ban of Benwick whose brother is Bors of Gaul. But he finds no place in early insular tradition. He seems to come from the continent and be familiar initially only to continental storytellers.

Benwick has not been identified: Malory recorded beliefs about Bayonne and Beaune, clearly placing Benwick in France. But, if we are looking for a genuine historical figure, it may be worth considering the name of Lancelot's British castle: Joyous Gard. Malory records beliefs that this corresponded to Alnwick or Bamborough Castle[*] on the north-east coast. That's as may be. *But there is a Breton castle of that name.*

On the edge of the river Elorn in the forest of Landerneau in north-western Brittany are to be found the fragmentary traces of the ancient Château de la Joyeuse-Garde (marked on modern maps as well as by the 17th century Blaeu). When Angustus Hare visited it over a century ago, only a Gothic vault and a 12th century gateway remained. He remarked that these ruins were almost all that were left to the great house of Rohan out of their whole principality of Léon.

The early history of this Château is unknown to me,

---

[*] In Berneich (Bernicia), which might possibly be the original of Benwick.

and while it may have been a folly or its current name added subsequently,[*] its foundations at least may take us back to a much more ancient history, especially if there is any truth in the following tale.

In the Life of St Tenenan, an Irishman named as a pupil of Carantoc, the charming early 17th century cleric Albert Le Grand gives us one apparent glimpse of very early events: the Danes have been ravaging the Léon countryside, and the surviving inhabitants have fled to secure or secret locations. The vessel of the saint is seen sailing up the river, and the sentinel on duty at the château, which has been garrisoned and strengthened by the locals, cries out that their saviour is arriving. A cry of joy is heard from the château garrison by the others in the forest, who exclaim in their turn a Breton expression in response to the garrison: the words understood as Joyous Gard form part of their expression. St Tenenan comes ashore at Joyous Gard to great acclaim.

There is no Lancelot here nor any named owner of the château. But, while we do not have to believe in this origin of its name, the story makes the château out to be very ancient indeed if one of the early saints really visited it.

Might Lancelot have fled his home province north of Brest in the 450s for Britain? We know of terrible devastations wrought around Brest by invaders at that time. Might some district or township have been named after the river Benoit, north-west of the Chateau? (Plabennec still survives.) And might Bors of Gaul hide an

---

[*] Mallerstang Castle in Cumbria, built by one of Becket's murderers, Hugh de Morville in the 12th century, had its name changed to Pendragon at the beginning of the 14th.

original French expression 'bords de Galle(s)' i.e (at the) edge of Gaul?

It would be good to know the true identity of King Claudas, named as Ban and Bors' powerful and dangerous opponent. According to which part of Arthur's life Lancelot might have belonged to this is most likely Chlodio (King C.431- C.449) or Clovis (Chlodoveus) who ruled from 481 to 512, both leaders of the Franks. (Noteworthy are the Roman names of Ban and Bors' retainers).*

It is wrong to suggest that this is the only road to go down, however convincing it superficially appears. For instance, in the South Saxon Annals recorded in the A-S Chronicle, Wlenc makes his entrance in 477 with his father Aelle, subsequently giving his name to Lancing. Linchmere in Sussex (Wlenc's Lake) becomes of interest since Lancelot was called 'Du Lac', *Of the Lake*. There is also a Longslow in Shropshire, testifying to the burial place of a Wlanc.

---

* I have mentioned elsewhere that Banw and Benwig figure as Arthur's followers in *Culhwch and Olwen*. Clovis is the more probable of the two kings since the climax of the Lancelot story has Gwenhwyfar at its epicentre.

Appendix 11 - Arthurian Sites in Devon

Though there are well-known sites in Cornwall and Somerset, Devon has been largely overlooked. The following may be of interest.

In Marie de France's Lay of Eliduc (already discussed) Eliduc arrives from Brittany into the realm of Totenois, 'for many kings dwell in that country, and ever there were strife and war.' Eliduc seeks out an old and powerful king near Exeter, who is having a bad time because he will not bestow his daughter upon one of his neighbours …

But, much more specifically, in Layamon's Brut - a version of Geoffrey's history - Cador [i.e Cadwy] pursues the Saxon Childric, first to Totnes, but ultimately to a great hill named Teinewic above the river Teine [Teign] and slaughters Childric and his army there. This site is markedly different from Geoffrey's Thanet. It is to be found at Highweek, outside Newton Abbot. While it suits the locale of the Duke of Cornwall better, we must not forget the gift of Teignweek to Lucan the Butler (see Preface). To some extent, Layamon's choice of site may be based on the similarity of names between his and Geoffrey's settings.

I have already mentioned Arthur's "quoit" matches, both in my own neighbourhood and at Moretonhampstead, the eastern gateway onto Dartmoor; and likewise his Seat and Oven, though there are other candidates for the seat. If I am right in believing the monks travelled via Buckfast Abbey before arriving at Tavistock then the one I have chosen is surely the correct site.

On the southern coast, in that beautiful and enclosed region, the South Hams, we find a site for Camlan. It is the environs of Slapton Ley, a body of fresh water, now a

Arthurian Sites in Devon | 171

nature reserve, only yards from the sea, divided from it simply by its own shoreline, a road, and Slapton Sands. This may be the site that inspired Tennyson in 'Idylls of the King'. For he stayed at Salcombe nearby, having been invited down by his friend J.A. Froude, the historian. The setting is inspirational. But it is not clear that the legend goes back beyond Tennyson's time, if that far. However, Slapton Ley is in the heart of Dumnonia, and a departure by water would not be a problem - though this is the wrong coast for Glastonbury. A short sea-journey east from Slapton Sands (where the French landed and were defeated at the beginning of the 15th century) leads us, at a distance of some 3-4 miles, to Dartmouth.

This anciently splendid port and harbour was long ago superseded by Plymouth so that its historic importance can be understated.

As a major export point for moorland tin and other materials this would have been a main destination for sea traffic comparable to Bantham on the western side of Dartmoor. It stands at the mouth of the Dart estuary running down from Buckfast and Staverton and through Totnes.*

The body of Earl Beorn betrayed by his kinsman was brought ashore here in 1049/50, perhaps at Bayard's Cove, and 'buried deep' before its transferral to Winchester to be placed beside Beorn's uncle, King Canute.

Here also the abbess Cuniburga perhaps superintended a nunnery three centuries earlier, giving her name to what

---

* One of which may represent the Derventio Statio of the Ravenna Cosmographer - another indication of the river's commerce. But it should be added that that no evidence for Dark Age tinning on Dartmoor has yet been clearly identified.

became latterly Bow Creek. (The earlier name Hunbergefleot appears to commemorate her).

Perhaps also Kingswear on the opposite bank commemorates a king who lived by fishing - a Fisher King, whose stronghold might have lurked half-hidden amongst the trees in the clifftop surroundings. In the romances, Gawain visits one such castle at the mouth of a royal river. The Fisher King was through the connotations of his French description - 'pêcheur' meaning both fisherman and sinner - somewhat Christianized by the romancers, but his prosaic origins are evident: commercial fishing was the source of his wealth and prosperity.[*]

Lastly, in the north of the county, on the heights of Exmoor near Challacombe, and in sight of the sea, is sited the ancient earthwork known as Shoulsbarrow or Shoulsbury Castle, highest of all the Exmoor fortifications. One authority regards it as enjoying the finest view in North Devon.

Square in shape, its inner area covering some four acres, it retains on three sides vestiges of a rampart and ditch. Two swords, perhaps Roman - one having a hilt of gold - have been found here *inter alia.*

This has been named in folklore as an Arthurian stronghold, but Alfred is also supposed to have used it against the Danes.

The grim winter weather could scarcely have allowed for year-round occupation. Bleak and isolated amongst the surrounding hills, its dank vegetation swept by the winds, this was a brilliantly strategic, never a comfortable site.

---

[*] The old name of a pit or cave to the side of Kingswear Castle was King's Oven: another smelting house for tin? Or a smokehouse for a fishery?

Appendix 12 - "Quoit" Contests

The games of boulders, in which two adversaries hurl missiles at each other, and the consequence is a pile of rocks in the middle, seem to belong to remotest Celtic antiquity: My main text ends with one of those (between Arthur and the Devil) in my immediate neighbourhood; and, for instance, I could point to a further combat outside Moretonhampstead only a few miles away involving Heltor, Hingstone rocks and, in between, (I believe) Blackingstone Rock.* In Brittany lived giants in the Monts d'Arrée, one group in Plouyé, one in Berrien. They hated each other. Their boulders ended up in the fascinating Chaos of Huelgoat, which even after the terrible flood disaster of a few years ago, remains a charming destination. I do not doubt that originally it was a single giant for each village engaged in combat.

This legend (to explain rock piles?)† seems to have developed from boulders into the use of quoits, and there is an instance of at least one battle involving steel balls: At Dinas Emrys in Nant Gwynant, Owen, the reputed son of Maxen (= Magnus Maximus) is said to have fought with a giant using these and paid with his life. (In a more dubious version of the story the giant is named as Urnach.). This story was recorded in 1693 and is said by Rachel Bromwich to relate to other "giant" folklore in MS Pen. 118. (C.1600). But the interest for me is that when my friend the red-haired Edgar F - was staying in my house 20

---

* The tomb of the giant Maximagur (Maxen Vawr?) may be found close by on Mardon Down. He may have been one of the original combatants.

† I remember my headmistress of long ago, Florence Gates telling me how she thought of thunder and lightning as giants playing ninepins.

years ago he came down in the morning troubled by a strange dream about fighting with an unknown assailant. Their weapons were steel balls.

A more modern version of the quoits combat was recorded by Georges Monot in the early years of last century, he having heard it at Loctudy in Brittany:

A dispute arose between three friends (or brothers) St Tudy, St Tual and St Vennec, during a game of *galoche* (of the quoits kind), about where they should exercise their ministries without mutual interference. They decided to throw their quoits to identify their respective areas. Beginning with St Tudy, each one surpassed the previous thrower; the consequent spheres of influence being each derived from the landing-points of the (impossibly large) throws of the competitors.

Appendix 13 - Two further combats: Mont St Michel and Mount Ar(a)wy

The romances contain a number of battles in which Arthur is present, but it is very difficult to distinguish pure fiction from some kind of historical reality. It is after an unnamed battle linked with the siege of Bedegraine Castle in Sherwood Forest, for example, that Leonora (Lionors) comes to do homage to Arthur: they fall in love, she bears a son, Borre, and then Arthur is off to help Ogyrfan (Leodegrance) in Cabeiliauc (Cameliard) against Rience of North Wales and meets Guinevere. This is Malory's version but it seems the wiser course to stick with Geoffrey: lost sources or ancient traditions are more likely with him.

We have looked at Arthur's battles with Flollo and Lucius Hiberius in the main text. But what are we to make of Arthur's defeating a giant at Mont - St - Michel?[*]

The answer seems to lie in the name of the king's niece he comes to rescue: Helena. For the name of a very small island (where someone actually managed to eke out an existence at the end of the 19th century close by the mount) is Tombelaine. This clearly suggested to Geoffrey or his source Tumba Helenae as its origin, the Tomb of Helen; and his story grew around this. But we now believe it was Tumba Belini, the tomb of a Celtic god Bel or Beli and think it probable that the Mount was the god's first resting-place, the name Tombelaine being transferred when Christianity reached the Mount.

Much more intriguing is the reference to another encounter made by Arthur after he has defeated the giant:

---

[*] This is the giant of the country of Constantine mentioned in the Preface.

he says he has never found anyone so strong since killing the giant Retho on Mount Arawy (Aravius).

At once we think of Rheiddwn Arwy in *Culhwch and Olwen*. He is listed without any clues as to his identity and may possibly be the same as Rheiddwn son of Beli or even Rheiddwn son of Eli Adfer; and the father *might be* Eli, Arthur's own huntsman.

However, tradition takes us elsewhere. In a story of which the ultimate origins are unknown to me, but which figures in the 19th century Iolo Mss and in a mid-17th century version, the mad King Peibiaw of Ergyng, a portion of modern-day Herefordshire, had an absurd disagreement with a neighbouring king, Nynniaw.* At the

---

* Here is Percy's 17th century version in which the protagonists are brothers and not kings. One might be forgiven for thinking that Percy believed this to be a part of recent history. He says, 'it is not to be questioned for the truth thereof.'

Two entirely loving brothers upon occafion of recreation, walking one evening within the Precincts of their ordinary dwelling, and beholding the skie befpotted all over with ftars, one of them of a fudden wifhed as many fat Oxen of his own, as there appeared little lights in the Firmament; the other again, not to be behind hand with his brother as he thought in invention, alfo defired Paftorage as large as the whole Element, and then demanded how his Cattel would be fed? the first apprehending belike indiscreetly some intention of affront to his vain-glorious conceits; in heat and choler told his brother that they should feed in his pasture, whether he would or no; wherefore the other being also moved with passion, at this seeming intention of compulsion, hastily replyed, that as by right he could not claim any interest in his Field or Medow, so was he fully resolved to debar him from all benefit and commodity therein. But in conclusion, from words they went to blowes, until at last both drawing out their weapons, which they had unfortunately about them, they soon became each others murtherer, before any of the house could come to their rescue, notwithstanding there wanted not good store of company in that noble family.

Two Further Combats | 177

end of a dreadful war that followed, Rhitta, king of North Wales, took advantage of the situation and defeated them both.

The mediaeval poet Elis o'r Nant knew of an ancient cairn on the top of Snowdon where Rhitta was said to be buried, as did the 19th century Lady Rhys. The cairn came to be known as Carnedd y Cawr, the Giant's Cairn, but a tower replaced it on the site, then a hotel. Rhys Goch Eryri, a poet who died C. 1420 wrote:

> On the ridge cold and vast,
> There the giant Ricca lies.

The name y wyddfa was specially applied to the mountain from its containing Rhitta's gwyddfa or mausoleum, supposedly constructed by each of his men placing a stone on it.

In Malory, we find Rience or Ryons of North Wales, believed to be the same man. (Less likely is Rica or Ricca who seems to have married Arthur's mother after Gorlwys his father's death: this Rica is referred to as one of the chief elders of Cornwall.) Rience has similar aggressive propensities.

But did Arthur kill him? It is surely a difficulty that Geoffrey's Mount Arawy appears distinct from Snowdon, which was also called Eryri, the place of eagles. Arawy and Eryri are difficult to equate, unlike Retho(n) and Rience, which, if we remove the 'th' as the French regularly were accustomed to, are virtually identical.

Before 1152, Suger, abbot of St Denys in France referred to Geoffrey's Merlin prophecies highlighting their extraordinary accuracy in relation to Henry I. He quotes as follows: 'There will succeed the lion of justice… his eagle will nest on Mount Arawy.' By seizing hold of Geoffrey's second mention of Mount Arawy, he surely implies he knows its whereabouts. And this would be in Normandy, for his account begins: 'At that time Henry I happened to come to the regions of the Normans...' But its location is not clear to us; while I myself am inclined to place Retho's defeat, where I believe Arthur was at the beginning of his career, in Brittany, and that therefore Arthur's Retho is a distinct figure from Rhitta, conflated by the similarity of their names. And for Mount Arawy I suggest the northern Breton range of the *Monts d'Arrée*.*

But, for those who believe Arawy and Eryri are one and the same, the evidence of the cairn on Snowdon cannot be disputed. Only the awkward question would remain: was Arthur involved in Rhitta's death?†

---

* The ancient form of the name in a Life of St Melor might be consistent with Aravius. Its summit is *another* Mont-St-Michel.

[But Arwy (as in Rheiddwn Arwy) is harder to align. And in any case, do we believe Rheiddwn took his second name from the mountain where he died?]

This tale looks like a traditional piece of Welsh folklore picked up by Geoffrey, whether or not Arthur was originally included, but, since it is mentioned in connexion with the Tombelaine story, we cannot rule out its being in a French setting and from a Breton source.

† If Retho, Rhitta and Rience really are to be equated, at least Malory supplies a realistic motive for the killing, as recorded at the start of this appendix.

Appendix 14 - Arthurian Artefacts

Arthur's sword, and the inscribed cross from his supposed tomb have been mentioned already. My suggestion about the wax seal of which the inscription was shown to the Imperial ambassador in 1531 is as follows: that it was created by the German merchants as a gift for Richard of Cornwall in the mid-13th-century, the text based on Arthur's achievements as recorded by Geoffrey; no doubt, there was a story of its "discovery" that came with it. Its purpose would be to remind Richard, king Henry III's brother, of Britain's glorious past, and his own right to rule the Holy Roman Empire, where there was currently a vacancy. Richard's subsequent attempt to become Emperor was not ultimately successful, though his rule was recognized within a limited area. Having squandered a great deal of money - he was the wealthiest man in Europe, which was why he was chosen - he was unable to secure the papal blessing and retired defeated of his purpose. I suggest he placed the seal in King Edward the Confessor's newly created shrine at Westminster sometime after this. But it might not be easy to determine exactly why.[*]

There was also Arthur's crown, 'held in highest honour over a long period by the Welsh.' This was offered to Edward I in 1283, according to the Waverley Annals, the spoils of his successful warfare. Llewelyn the Great, who died in 1240, was amongst the Welsh rulers said to have worn it.

The crystalline cross allegedly given to Arthur by the

---

[*] Or Richard himself had it created to support his claim. (It might even have come out of Edward I's Welsh treasure.)

Virgin Mary and kept at Glastonbury Abbey, according to John of Glastonbury, and the Winchester Round Table (still surviving) might also be mentioned.

To the Welsh, the most sacred of the treasures captured by Edward I was the Crosnaid, the Cross of Destiny, believed to have been brought back to Britain by the emperor Constantine's mother Helena. This was supposedly a fragment of the True Cross, to which gems and a gold overlay were subsequently added. It is traceable in England to the 15th century and was sought for in 1982, with what results I do not know. There is no obvious connexion of any kind with the Wedale fragments (see Cap 19) nor the crystalline cross abovementioned.

Appendix 15 - Parley to Violence: The Raid of the Reidswire

The raid of the Reidswire is a distressing instance of a parley gone wrong. The Scots and English had one of their periodic meetings on July 7th, 1575 to settle border disputes. Both sides appeared to be on the best of terms, but 'no one could have suspected that so much bad feeling was hidden under a fair exterior, and ready to burst forth in a moment with volcanic fury.'

The two wardens, Sir John Carmichael for the Scots, and Sir John Foster (Forrester) for the English, started arguing about a notorious English freebooter - Foster was requested to "play fair". Indignantly he raised himself in his saddle, and pointing at Carmichael told him to match himself with his equals.

> Carmichael bade them speik out plainlie,
> And cloke no cause for ill nor good;
> The other, answering him as vainlie,
> Began to reckon kin and blood:
> He raise, and raxed him where he stood,
> And bade him match with him his marrows;
> Then Tindaill heard them reason rude,
> And they loot off a flight of arrowes.

The fight started badly for the Scots but, because of plundering by the men of Tyndale who thought they (the English) could not be beaten, and the unexpected arrival of Scotsmen with fire-arms from nearby Jedburgh, the English were routed, with Sir John Heron killed, and Foster and others of rank taken prisoner. They were sent into custody in Dalkeith till the Earl of Morton dismissed them with presents of falcons.

Elizabeth the First was very angry and sent the Earl of Huntingdon to meet Morton on the borders. Morton made enough concessions to calm the situation, and Carmichael was briefly imprisoned at York. But he was dismissed with honour when closer investigation showed Foster to be at fault, and goods forfeited by the Scots were returned to them.

It was a very ugly incident where bad feeling stole the advantage over good sense. How many parleys involving armed men must have developed like this!

Appendix 16 - La Villemarqué's Rehabilitation

La Villemarqué's treasure house of ballads 'Le Barzhaz Breizh' was a tremendous success on its publication in 1839, while he was still in his early 20s. We may suspect envy amongst other ballad-collectors, to whom many of La Villemarqué's pieces were unknown. But then came the backlash beginning from an enlarged edition in 1867. Here is an account by the usually sensible Sabine Baring - Gould writing in 1901:

"In 1837 M. de la Villemarqué published his Barzas breiz, a collection that purported to be made from the lips of the Bretons of their traditional ballads, historical, legendary, and mythological.

The Barzas breiz was hailed with enthusiasm in France and was crowned by the Academy.

So years passed, and others, notably M. Luzel, began to collect. Then he found that what he gathered was not quite the same as what De la Villemarqué had given to the world, and that of some of the most interesting historical and poetical pieces not a trace could anywhere be discovered.

De la Villemarqué was an amiable and well intentioned man, and none suspected him of forgery. But what had taken place was this. He had largely "restored" ballads of which he had picked up mere fragments; he did this without indicating where his restorations came in. Worse than this, he had accepted a budget of contributions forwarded to him by at least one friend whom he trusted, and who had manufactured the pieces and passed them off on the uncritical and unsuspicious De La Villemarqué as genuine antiques.

He was not satisfied without giving to those pieces which he himself heard a fictitious antiquity. For instance, the Bretons have a song strictly like our familiar "Sing a song of One O! What shall I sing you?"

Now, de la Villemarqué touched it up, adding lines of his own to convert it into a Druidic lesson imparting deep mysteries to a pupil. Not a word of this occurs in the genuine ballad.

The Barzas breiz, after having hoaxed the Academy and pretty nearly every English traveller in Brittany, who flies to it to extract padding for his volume of travels, has fallen into disrepute; and although the learned are unwilling to say hard words of a man who sought to popularise the ballads of his native land and dealt with them in a stupid manner, they can trust to the genuineness of no single piece in the collection unless its counterpart can be found in the volumes of M. Luzel.

De la Villemarqué should have named his authorities and have indicated what alterations he had introduced into the text, and should have left copies of the ballads as he received them. But he had the example of such men as Bishop Percy and Sir Walter Scott before him, and he followed their traces. He has been termed the Macpherson of Brittany."

So La Villemarqué, a charming man, was discredited. He never sought to defend himself, perhaps deeming himself inferior in scholarship to his critics, and aware of the amateur nature of some of his methods.

La Villemarqué died and still the attacks went on. These culminated in a horribly hostile, massive work by Francis Gourvil published in 1960. But at last help was at hand. Along comes the delightful young scholar Donatien Laurent who, on a memorable day in 1964, rediscovered the lost manuscript notebooks in the La Villemarqué

Château. These manuscripts were not complete, but now La Villemarqué's methods could be properly studied, and it was impossible to doubt these were recordings in his rushing hand made in the presence of the ballad reciters. Laurent's first book on the subject, Aux Sources Du Barzaz-Breiz, was published to acclaim in 1989. We must hope there is more to come. And, for all his amateurishness (reflecting the standards of the time), La Villemarqué was largely exonerated. Here were the ballads direct from the lips of the people, sometimes in obscure old Breton that La Villemarqué, perhaps not understanding, mistakenly updated. Laurent has triumphantly answered La Villemarqué's critics. The Barzhaz Breizh can now be justly reclaimed as a masterpiece of Breton literature, one that draws upon the cultural memory of countless generations.[*]

---

[*] Baring-Gould's comments upon *Sing a song of One O!* and La Villemarqué's untrustworthy friend are of course to be taken into account. The full story is yet to be told.

Appendix 17 - On the Genuineness of Cian's Prophecy

Unlike, for instance, the Merlin cycle of verses or *The Plague of Elliant*, of which the original text survives (as given by the ballad-reciter) Cian's Prophecy has the misfortune to be without any manuscript authority, though there are pages missing towards the beginning and end of the first notebook that might once have contained it. It is difficult to believe they will ever turn up.

La Villemarqué has been revealed as an embroiderer or *mender* of damaged or incomplete texts but never as a fabricator of non-existent ones. But is the Prophecy an exception - or *the* exception? Let us first take note of the following exchange with the academic ballad-collector, Luzel in August or September of 1867, he having been invited to dinner along with the abbé Henry by La Villemarqué:

Luzel:- I hold the conviction that it is you who have composed the oldest pieces in the Barzhaz Breizh.

La Villemarqué, hiding his head in his hands: - O! You make me sick when you say that to me. Nothing can give me greater distress than hearing such things.

Luzel:- However, that is my conviction. I can only urge you to speak the truth about this.

La Villemarqué, indicating an old piece of furniture that had been restored, decorated with figurines and other carvings:- Do you see this old piece that I have restored? Well, I have done for the Barzhaz Breizh what I have done for the statuettes decorating it … I have put legs on some, arms on others.

:- And heads on others! exclaimed the abbé Henry.

La Villemarqué was a teenager when he began to form his collection of ballads. Could he have been guilty of a jeu d'esprit? We may remember that the young Prosper Mérimée's second book The Guzla published in 1827 was a spoof collection of poems of Illyria with wild and dramatic tales of vampires and suchlike.

But against such reservations we may note that Clémence Penquerc'h who died in 1908 was *very* familiar with the Prophecy, though conceivably she had obtained knowledge of it from La Villemarqué's book. And, more importantly, we have evidence that La Villemarqué's own grandmother, herself a ballad-collector, also had knowledge of it.* Donatien Laurent, perhaps in the best position of all to judge, has declared: 'At least, the probabilities of this text having existed seem to me serious, contrary to the opinions of Luzel, Loth and F. Gourvil.'

I do not know the precise factors leading to the collapse of the oral tradition at this time, but suppose that better and more frequent transport, and more regular news supply would be amongst them.

In Britain, at almost the same moment, Robert Hunt was collecting traditional stories. He has this to say about the period, in his introduction to 'Popular Romances of the West of England':

'Mrs Bray collected her Traditions, Legends and Superstitions of Devonshire in 1835, and they were published in 1838. This work proves to me that even at that time the old-world stories were perishing *like the shadows on the mist before the rising sun.* Many wild tales which I heard in 1829 appear to have been lost in 1835.'

And, elsewhere, he writes as follows:

'I cannot but consider myself fortunate in having

---

* Is it conceivable that a scholar transcribed it from the Landévennec ms and gave it to the ballad-reciters?

collected these traditions thirty-five years ago. They could not be collected now. Mr J. O. Halliwell speaks of the difficulties he experienced in his endeavours to obtain a story. The common people think they will be laughed at if they tell their "ould drolls" to a stranger. Beyond this, many of the stories have died out with those who told them. In the autumn of 1862, being very desirous of getting every example of folk-lore which existed in the remote parishes of Zennor and Morva, I employed the late C. Taylor Stephens, "sometime rural postman from St Ives to Zennor," and the author of "The Chief of Barat-Anac," to hunt over the district. This he did with especial care, and the results of his labours are included in those pages. The postman and poet, although he spent many days and nights amidst the peasantry, failed to procure stories which had been told me, without hesitation, thirty years before.'

The cultural isolation so favourable to the oral tradition could seldom, as in the following story, be exemplified as late as 1854. A London visitor to the westcountry arrives at the remote (and now lost) village of Hallsands on the coast of South Devon:

'Here, as everywhere else, What news about the [Crimean] war? was the first question. Mine, *already a week old*, was news at Halsands ...'

Appendix 18 - La Villemarqué's other ballads

In addition to the two ballads translated in this work, it is worth mentioning a number of others covering events roughly from the Arthurian period.

The Submersion of Caerys relates how the daughter of King Gradlon the Great undid sophisticated precautionary measures prepared against the sea for Gradlon's capital city; from which cause the city was destroyed. (The unknown settlement of Chris is mentioned in one Roman record.)[*]

The Wine of the Gauls and *The Dance of the Sword* beginning 'White grape wine is better than blackberry …', in which blood is gorily interspersed amongst the wine, is really two songs combined. The first concerns Breton raids into Gallic territory to thieve their wine. La Villemarqué believed it referred to 6th century invasions of Frankish territory, probably around Nantes where white wine was produced.

The Pestilence of Elliant beginning 'Between Langolen and Le Faouet lives a holy bard called Father Ratian…' concerns the dreadful plague (which carried off Maelgwn). While Elliant itself suffered terribly, the neighbouring area in Cornouaille was saved by Ratian's prayers.

Four fragments of a Merlin cycle of verses include Merlin's conversion to Christianity by Saint Kado.

The Legend of Saint Ronan concerns his illtreatment at the hands of a woman called Keban, in the reign of

---

[*] 'Sixty-seven mantles of scarlet (and then some) would leave the town of Ys for mass at Lanval.' (Old Breton saying)

Gradlon.*

Saint Efflamm and King Arthur is primarily concerned with a (British) prince and his saintly Irish wife, the princess Enora. He goes to Brittany, which 'was then ravaged by wild animals and dragons desolating all the province, and especially the countryside of Lannion. Many of them had been slain by the Bretons' supreme commander Arthur ...' He helps Arthur kill a wild beast. The ballad ends, 'To prevent one's forgetting these things which have never been consigned to any book, I have put them into verse to be sung in the churches.' These churches are thought to be Plestin, site of the tomb of Efflamm, and Perroz-Guirec which has a sculpted image of Arthur's victory over a dragon from the beach of St-Michel-en-Gréve.† The bishop of Tréguier had the body of

---

* Gradlon has his own interest. In the Landévennec Cartulary we find many mentions of a Gradlon 'king of the Bretons and part of the Franks'. Other mentions include a Frankish embassy coming to seek help from him against an indeterminate enemy and giving him 40 Frankish 'civitates' so that he must have ruled over the Franks like Ambrosius. But there are several Gradlons including one whose capital was Quimper, probably in the time of Arthur's stay. Poetry preserved in Wrdisten's 9th century Life of Winwaloe records how Gradlon, 'when the enemy race was laid low after the barbarian wars, defeated the 'Keels' of five chiefs and cut off their heads ... Let my witness be the river Loire, by whose fair banks so many battles were then so keenly fought'. The enemy here would appear to be Saxon, and it is intriguing to speculate on Arthur's own involvement, though the dating of these events hinges upon the meaning of 'the barbarian wars'. We owe a debt to the learned, literary Wrdisten who was (I believe) responsible for the preservation of Cian's text over many centuries. Cian's Prophecies may have been modernized in his time from an ancient and obscure version.

† Geoffrey might have merged this story with the name of Tombelaine to create a different combat and setting.

Efflamm removed to Plestin in 999. La Villemarqué notes Tréguier's particular affection for Arthur excelled by no other district.

Lastly, *The Tower of Armor* concerns the tribulations of Azénor, a saint and princess, the daughter of Audren, chief of the Armorican Bretons who was supposed to have founded the town of Châtel-Audren. Azénor's son Budok was also a saint. Audren is probably the same leader as the Breton mentioned by Geoffrey under the name Aldroenus.

Appendix 19 - The Battle of Saint-Cast

There are many treats in La Villemarqué's wonderful store of ballads, and not least is Number 47 - Le Combat de Saint-Cast.

In September 1758 the British descended upon Saint-Cast, west of Dinard in northern Brittany, seeking to protect channel routes and divert France from hostilities with Germany, Britain's allies. In the preliminaries to the battle, Breton soldiers from Tréguier and Saint Pol-de-Léon advanced towards a detachment of Welsh mountainmen singing a song: the Bretons halted in astonishment, for they knew it well. They 'intoned the patriotic refrain'. Now it was the Welsh turn to freeze. An order given by commanding officers on both sides to fire was ignored. Both sides threw down their arms and 'renewed on the battlefield the brotherly ties uniting their forefathers'. This was told La Villemarqué by the grandson of one of those present, and a subsequent researcher, M. de Saint-Pern, had heard it from several other credible persons; he also declared it was a traditional folktale in the countryside. This battle was not a British success, but it is not possible to say what effect the incident had upon what followed.

I am reminded of the fraternization of the British and Germans on Christmas day, 1914 at the beginning of the 1st World War. Surely I am correct in believing that the Germans led the way in this, and that they were a regiment from Saxony. In the 2nd World War, an old friend, William Skinner of Strete fought in North Africa and was taken prisoner, at Tobruk (I think). He was sent back to a German P.O.W camp in Saxony where the Saxons from outside used to come and pass chocolate and cigarettes to the prisoners with expressions such as: 'For we are brothers'. Sadly the English have never honoured these ties.*

---

* The Saxons seem to have had a main hand though others, especially Bavarians, followed suit. There were a number of incidents around this time e.g: 'In November [1915] a small fraternization occurred ... *again initiated by the Saxons* ...' (Silent Night - S Weintraub). What I wish to suggest is that Saxon goodwill was the original trigger for these peaceful episodes.

A POSTSCRIPT (In The Form Of A Response To Two Recent Publications)

At a late stage in the preparation of this book, I discovered *Concepts of Arthur* by Thomas Green (2007) and *Worlds of Arthur* by Guy Halsall (2012). These volumes, radically different from one another and from my own, were of great interest.

Green denies Arthur's existence, in a cogent and crystal-clear thesis demanding great respect. Obviously *inter alia* his point of view cannot countenance any historical validity for the battle-list. A few further points regarding the battle-sites seem to be called for.

To equate these battles with battles recorded elsewhere is intriguing but unproven. Thus, Green may be right to posit that Celidon Wood is the same as the fictional battle of Cat Goddeu, though I doubt it; the 6th century battle at the Cells of Brewyn recorded by Taliesin may be the same battle as Agned Cat Breguoin - I think the approximate sites *are* the same - but two battles can be fought at the same place,* as I think is also the case with Urbs Legionis, the city of the Legion: another battle recorded by the Annales Cambriae for 613 happened here, at Chester. But why necessarily *the same* battle? Similarly there was a battle (bellum) Badonis (of Mount Badon?) recorded by the Annales for 665. But here it is specifically mentioned as being *secundo*, for the second time.†

---

* However, Taliesin resists the opportunity to make any comparison between the victor, his adored patron Urien of Rheged, and the older hero.

† If we follow the annalist the battles have the same location - probably in the south-west, judging by the 2nd battle. Another double location from the Annales is Mount Carno - 728, and again (apparently) in 951.

Traeth Tribruit, shore of (the river) Tribruit, is very probably not only the Historia Brittonum's battle but one mentioned in an apparently Scottish context involving Bedwyr, according to an early poem. If the poetic battle is fought against dog-heads (werewolves?) are we therefore to dismiss the battle as genuinely historical out of hand? An historical affair may have been subsequently mythologized by story-tellers. Or there may have been a wolf-cult of warriors in the north.

For one of these battles the compiler gives the British name: Cat Coit Celidon and, for a second, an early gloss or variant text adds: Cat Breguoin. The second is particularly intriguing because we have a double identification.

And what of the remaining four (or seven) battles? Dubglas, Bassas, Guinnion and Glein. I believe the 4-verse theory to account for Dubglas is a good one i.e. four verses of a poem commemorating a single battle being misunderstood as commemorating four battles. But what is particularly appealing is that *we have no other references to any of these*. They are certainly at least as probably historical as they are legendary or mythological. To my mind this adds to their credibility. I take no particular account of Green's finding *Linnuis* to be an early 9th century form. In the first place, Nennius may have updated an earlier form or he may have been speaking out of personal knowledge. But Green's theory depends upon an unproven belief that it refers to the people of Lindsey, who probably would be said to live in a regnum (kingdom), not a regio (district or region). There is also no river Douglas in Lindsey.[*]

While perfectly willing to accept that these battles

---

[*] Reading Luinnuis, the people of the Lune (river), we might consider the river Douglas north-west of Wigan.

may not necessarily have been drawn from a single poem, they carry for me the hallmarks of a genuine and honest attempt by the compiler to provide historical information. That is, he may have included this or that unhistorical battle, but I doubt very much he sought to pull the wool over our eyes; he may have made mistakes, but he neither deliberately included mythological or legendary material - nor fabricated.

Green suggests that two of the cities in the city-list are likewise from mythology: Caer *Urhnarc* and Caer *Celemion*. Again I reply that Green may be right, probably *is*, but that this brings no discredit upon the compiler's conscientious and honest efforts. For I believe he thought them genuine.

I make no attempt to deny my admiration for Green's statement of the negative case. There is so much to consider in the positions on every issue that he takes up. In broad terms, he sees a hero of mythology historicized and discovers clues to the mythical figure's origins. He even suggests tentatively that Arthur was once a Celtic god.

He shows how in the Breton Life of Efflam, the 12th century author is clearly modelling Arthur on Hercules, and that in a 12th or 13th century Irish tale, Arthur's Irish counterpart Finn conquers him in an expression of two rival cultures and mythologies. Obviously I come from another position, believing that an historical figure was subsequently mythologized by some - even to the point of his historicity being doubted.

Guy Halsall favours an archaeological approach and is uncomfortably dismissive of our literary sources which he tends to see as unreliable. He does not support the idea of a swift breakdown of the Roman administration after Constantine's rebellion nor of significant bloodshed. In fact he believes that an ethnic divide between the British and the incomers was pretty much non-existent and that they quickly learned to live side by side quite happily. I find this attitude frankly baffling, but, in the absence of archaeological findings to support the contrary view, I suppose I must accept where Halsall is coming from. However, if he reads Gildas' statement on the *divortium* (resulting in no-go areas when Gildas wrote)[*] and remembers the subsequent lower-class status given to the British in Anglo-Saxon Law as well as the extraordinary lack of word transferrals from Brythonic, Halsall will surely see racism was rife and violence a probability.[†] I have recorded elsewhere my belief that post-Roman Britain was awash with blood, but, perhaps more accurately I might say, *with bloody episodes*, for the numbers involved may not have been huge, but the episodes were many. And sometimes perhaps the numbers *were* huge. From the A-S Chronicle, I take:

> The battle of Crayford -
> 4,000 British dead.
> The battle of Wippedsfleot -
> 12 British nobles dead
> *- and how many retainers?*
> The massacre of Pevensey -

---

[*] Possibly these zones were by agreement; but only the agreements to cede Kent and other territories to Hengest, and another presumed after Mearcraedesburn are known to us.

[†] The evident western retreat to Cornwall (i.e. land of the Corn-Welsh) and Wales (i.e. the land of the foreigners) makes this particularly clear. As do lonely British outposts indicated by placenames beginning 'Wal'. Denbury, in my own locality, 'the fortress of the men of Devon', is a typical instance of separateness. Bede recorded the general British animosity towards the English when he wrote his history.

> a settlement inside the
> Roman fort of Anderida (+refugees?)
> completely wiped out
> The battle of Natanleag -
> 5,000 British dead.

Or do we treat these numbers as fantasies? 12,000 has been doubted as the figure for the army Riothamus took to France. But how many soldiers would we expect him to take when fighting a nation (the Goths)? There are many battles recorded by both sides in the 5th and 6th centuries, and, though the numbers involved may not have been huge - there were about 300 on the British side at Catraeth - these were significant events with important consequences. Surely it happened just as one would expect, *since the British were scarcely likely to forfeit their land willingly.* Of course I accept that sometimes they fled and the land would have been occupied, so to speak, peacefully. I can only urge Halsall to take our literary sources more seriously. They are valuable lights onto a twilight world infinitely more obscure without them.

In passing, I must note that Halsall's comments upon S.G. Wildman's fascinating theory are rather sad. This man developed a wholly original idea based upon hostelries called 'The Black Horse', the source of this name being deeply obscure and perhaps very ancient. Wildman came to believe that Arthur's cavalry rode black horses and that 'The Black Horse' hostelries were only found in and around British border country and not deep inside British kingdoms nor within Saxon territory. Thus the sign of the Black Horse might have held significance for both sides at a certain very early period. I do not see such a theory as contemptible or 'daft'; and I also refrain from making any comment about Halsall's own theories relative to two chronological notes in the Historia Brittonum (pp. 204 ff) except that any creativity is (I suppose) to be commended, however bizarre.

In this volume I have striven for the positive case for Arthur's existence in the face of negativity expressed by Green and others and the indifference expressed by many including Halsall. Even the title of John Morris' book, *The Age of Arthur*, has come under attack because of Arthur's shadowy nature. And yet this is how popular tradition has it: that a leader called Arthur successfully repelled or defeated opponents in the post-Roman period. And we have clear evidence from an early 6th century source (Gildas) that such an event really did occur. His words are to be found before the Preface, but I shall repeat them: 'For the memory of so hopeless a collapse of the island and *its unlooked for rescue* stuck in the minds of those who witnessed both extraordinary events.' In his chapters 24 and (start of) 25, Gildas recreates for us a sense of the appalling British suffering. For him this was clearly very real. Gildas died in 570, we believe, and in a time of strong oral tradition, I cannot see how events of the early 5th century would largely elude him.[*]

One can hardly doubt that there was an incredible reversal of fortune for the beleaguered British sometime in the mid-5th century. We know that Ambrosius Aurelianus was deeply associated with this, replacing the dead Vortimer as leader of the resistance. But the man who (*pace* Halsall) broke free from the Vortigern faction in 436 was probably not the victor of Badon, some 40 or more years later. If we search for a name of this leader, only one

---

[*] In the 1980s my great-aunt had stories to tell me of her father born in 1826 including his stormy relations with his mother before he joined the East India Company in 1842.

springs to mind ...

Our list of early references to Arthur is by no means negligible. In addition to the Historia Brittonum's battle-list and two other references in the Mirabilia on Arthur's son and his dog, we find two references in 7th century poems as well as that in Aneirin's great work - sometimes doubted because it is not without interpolations. In the 10th century Annales Cambriae, we encounter Badon, and for the first time, Camlan.

Additionally, we have Gildas' mention of Badon (without his naming the victor); a mention of Bedwyr's Well in a 7th century poem; four separate men named Arthur, all from C.600; the very ancient poem on the battle of Llongborth; and even Cian's possible reference if we accept the authenticity of his Prophecy.[*]

All these would predate William the Chaplain's Life of Goeznou (1019). William's own long reference to Arthur may depend on a lost Breton history. One might add that the Historia Brittonum contents list, compiled separately, is apparently the first to name Arthur as king.

Arthurians have little to complain of. We ask ourselves: where should we expect to find Arthur where his name is lacking? The second half of the 5th century is badly covered by any literary evidence. Gildas might have named him but chose not to - he hardly names anyone.[†] The fragments of 5th century history in the A-S Chronicle fail to name a single British opponent after 455 (= 434),

---

[*] There are probably no direct references to Arthur in Cian's Prophecies or surely, while the manuscript existed, some scholar would have dug them out.

[†] The omission of Arthur is bound to remind us of 'the dangers faced by most valiant soldiers in a grim war' - the story Gildas elected not to tell.

not even Ambrosius; in fact, only one, Natanleod, up to 571. And Bede is scarcely better, though including Ambrosius out of Gildas' text.

I am bound to draw attention to the 10th century Welsh poem, The Prophecy of Britain. Here, in a longish work, the anonymous author urges his Welsh compatriots to stand up against the heavy English taxation being imposed by the Cirencester stewards of Wessex. He imagines the Welsh rising under the leadership of Cynan and Cadwaladr. Both of these are to be thought of as past heroes fighting against the English.

Cadwaladr was son of Cadwallon of Gwynedd who defeated Edwin of Northumbria in 633 and was briefly Northumbria's ruler. Cadwaladr's death a generation after was mourned as the end of British hopes of regaining English land. Geoffrey ends his work with the reign of Cadwaladr. Cynan's historical place is uncertain. He may have been a brother or general of Cadwaladr's.[*] His very obscurity makes us want to cry out: but why not include Arthur? Such a question is unanswerable. Perhaps stories were already so prevalent about him that this 10th century author simply did not believe he was a genuine historical figure. Arthur's absence remains, however, a little surprising.[†]

---

[*] Geoffrey says, amongst Merlin's Prophecies recorded in the 7th Book of his History that Cadwaladr will summon *Conan*. He is possibly being influenced by the earlier prophetic work but may himself be meaning Conan Meriadoc, the legendary hero who carved out a kingdom in Brittany.

[†] The 12 surviving 6th century poems of Taliesin eulogize his own contemporary patrons. There are few retrospective references such as that to Agricola, Vortiporius' father contemporary with Arthur. This king, a famous warrior according to Taliesin, and good man according to Gildas, surely fought beside Arthur.

Geoffrey's book, while supplying a great many "facts" about Arthur's life leaves us in doubt about pretty much everything. If we take Arthur's birth at Tintagel, for example, independent evidence indicates that one of his mother's sisters married a Cornishman, and another a Breton. So, with an obscure Cornish hill-fort apparently preserving his father's name, I feel a western Dumnonian (north-eastern Cornish) origin not unlikely for him, especially if we believe Geoffrey had access to genealogical information lost to us. (We may also note that a (later?) husband of Arthur's mother is named an elder of Cornwall, in *Culhwch and Olwen*.) There is no counter-tradition, and Tintagel is a model site for defensibility such as a chieftain would have chosen. It was also occupied in this period, and much foreign ware has been found there. We might also mention the Arthnou stone (from a slightly later period), and Arthur's Cornish home, Celli Wig, at an unknown site, probably some distance to the west, in a later period of his life. Belief in the probability of Eigr's being his mother is provided by our awareness that he was fostered out, after his father's death (it would seem), to someone named in an early reference as his mother's first cousin. But this is, of course all circumstantial. It does not *prove* that he was born at Tintagel because Geoffrey is unreliable and is perfectly happy to embroider things as he goes along.

In this work I do not claim to have offered more than a working model for Arthur's biography based on what seemed to me, within the realms of plausibility and probability, acceptable. I have felt free to look askance at Arthur's great pitched battle at Vallis Siesia. This name may disguise a real battle near Aegidius' capital, Soissons. But it is at least as likely to be a "stolen" 754 battle-site (Vallis Seusana - or, Siusiana?) where the Frankish king

Pippin defeated Aistulf king of the Lombards. (Fredegar. IV. 37).

This is no different from saying that Arthur and his entourage - amounting to a kind of private army - may be derived from the mythological Finn and his Irish companions or equally from Arthur's own youthful observation of the Bacaudae, the French and Spanish travelling bands.

Any peruser of this work can see what importance I attach to the Arthurian names. I make no apology, considering them seriously undervalued. For instance, I believe a Merovingian king is concealed behind the name Flollo, and since the said king fits neatly into the chronology and politics and geography and no surviving source uses this form of the name, I have speculated that Geoffrey had a lost source which may have also indicated Arthur in opposition to the king. But again I do not wish to claim any kind of certainty about this.

Nor have I *proved* that Leonora's father Sevain is the same as Sefyn i.e. Kenyr, but it seems to me highly likely. Early manhood in Brittany would help to explain why, in the British tradition, Arthur is never less than leader. I take pleasure in finding credible information in late sources, however much this may be anathema to conventional historians. Because of a strong oral tradition and equally because of lost sources, we dare not simply pooh-pooh *possible information* to which no early date can be attached. Robert Graves reckoned there were genuine traditions about the Trojan War in the writings of 'Dictys' and 'Dares' not to be found in the Homeric works of many, many centuries earlier. (This may help to explain why I have even used a source as late as 1525(See cap.9.))*

Geoffrey Ashe formerly indicated a tradition about a Scandinavian of very ancient times (and long before Arthur) only verified recently. The oak at Hoxne, against which Edmund the 10th century king of the East Angles was allegedly shot to death by the Danes, was found in the 1840s to contain an arrowhead at its centre. The 19th century Somerset fishermen, who threw a stone upon a cairn before setting out and chanted "Inna Picwinna, give me a good dinner", appear to have been appealing to an early 8th century king of Wessex with the title *Pehtwyn* (friend of the Picts) that may not otherwise survive from that distant time. Nor should we forget the tradition of a descent from Vortigern recorded by the sweetshop ladies.†

Such examples encourage us to show respect to traditions, *even if we cannot verify them*, until we have the strongest grounds for dismissing them. There is plenty of feeble and absurd material in the Saints' lives, for instance, but the meeting claimed between Illtud and Arthur is plausible, as is the idea that Illtud received a military commission. It is not automatically a piece of nonsense and must be considered as a possible event between the two cousins probably already known to one another.

It remains an odd fact that the four people named Arthur, all found at roughly the end of the 6th or

---

* Recently Gildas' source for the Martyrdom of St Alban has resurfaced, while Morris points out reasons for believing the 11th century Rhigyfarch had access to a copy of the lost 6th century Rule of St David.

† Aelfthryth (see Cap. 2) was stepmother to King Edward enthroned in 975. Tradition records her as giving the orders for, or actually perpetrating his murder in 978 at Corfe Castle, where *the exact site* of his death would in recent times be (and is?) pointed out.

beginning of the 7th century, are with one exception of Irish stock. We cannot say why this curious phenomenon occurred at that time nor why the British failed to use Arthur's name for their children. But at least it appears to indicate significant interest in some recent figure. It is also not unlikely, in the case of the Arthur from the family of Gildas' south-Welsh tyrant Vortiporius, that one or two of his ancestors fought alongside Arthur, for these were not among the Irish expelled from Wales. Irish story-telling had its own impact upon Arthurian legend even (it would seem) to the naming of Arthur's sword, Excalibur and perhaps to Arthur's early opponent, Twrch Trwyth. In a land of mixed cultures this might be what we would expect, marriage especially being a unifying force between different traditions.

I do not really know how much, particularly out of the pleasantly confusing burden of sundry story-tellers, we can hope to recover of the true history of Arthur. Probably not very much. I have laboured to create a 3-dimensional figure but have mostly failed. I still believe the effort was worthwhile to attempt to rescue an heroic British warrior from historical oblivion. Commonsense surely insists on my correctness, but I cannot deny that the strictness of academic rigour may offer another view entirely. If there is a baby anywhere amongst the bathwater - and it is difficult to say otherwise authoritatively - I cannot doubt nor wish to that the search will go on. After all, so many questions remain without clear answers.

- Did Geoffrey's sourcebook in the British language really exist?
- Was Nennius aware of Gildas' text and, if so, why didn't he use it? (It was presented to the world 300 years before Nennius' time).

- Why did Nennius make Arthur so important? (Halsall points out that the Arthurian section is written as a chiasmus, a kind of purple passage, precisely 240 words long.) Was Arthur an obvious choice over other and more recent warrior heroes?
- What caused the extraordinary recovery recorded by Gildas (though he tempers this by saying the enemy had their share of victories before Badon)?
- Were there British cavalry?
- Why are the battlelist battles almost all otherwise unknown?
- Who won Badon?
- What happened at Camlan?
- Who was Riothamus?
- Was William of Malmesbury wrong to give Gwalchmei (Gawain) historical credibility?

This list could go on almost indefinitely. For instance, in what numbers did the Romans survive in Britain? Gildas is clearly wrong to posit Ambrosius as perhaps the last of them,* though he must have been unaware of Romans in his own time - despite knowing Ambrosius' grandson. (This suggests a swift Roman absorption into the British populace, much as we would expect.)

In our time we have seen, in what might be deemed similar circumstances, a number of white farmers clinging amid mayhem and murder to their farms in Zimbabwe, the good feeling, such as potentially generated by Ambrosius' leadership and successes, being entirely lacking.

---

* This belief might be taken as evidence that Gildas did not think of Arthur as a Roman.

The following details were recorded in *The Independent* for November 6th, 2013:

'About 18 white farmers were killed in violent takeovers of their land while almost all of the 620,000 farm-workers were driven from their homes' ... 'Together with dependants, [the total was about] 2,000,000 [displaced]' ... '6,000 white farmers have been replaced by 245,000 Zimbabwean farmers' ... 'Mr Mugabe [the president] said he embarked on the land-grab programme to address the expropriation of land from blacks during the 90 years of white rule that ended after a civil war ...'

To some of us, these and other conundrums will continue to offer a stimulating if tantalizing pleasure, while others may choose to believe the game is not worth the candle. In the celebrated words of a 17th century scholar, *What song the Syrens sang, or what name Achilles assumed when he hid himself among women, though puzzling questions, are not beyond all conjecture.*

THE ROYAL DYNASTY OF KENT

Saxon and British tradition concur on the names of the first leaders of the Saxons: Hengest and Horsa. But Horsa is a problematic figure. His name is, like Hengest's (Stallion), of a horsey kind: and it has been suggested that the alleged memorial to his death in fact contained the word 'Hors' from the Roman *Cohors* (cohort). Thomas Green points out the totemic use of the names Hengest and Horsa on the Continent.

Bede also has a counter-tradition that Hengest came with his son Oeric also known as Oisc. Oisc's importance is that he gave his name to the Kent dynasty Oiscingas. He is also, as Aesc, son of Hengest, found in the A-S Chronicle. He joins Hengest as fellow war-leader in 455 (= 434), six years after the Saxon arrival.

The Historia Brittonum tells us that Octa with his cousin Ebissa came south from their territory held in the north after his father Hengest's death. I do not doubt Hengest's existence, but I believe it was actually Oeric who was Octa's father, the dynasty being traced from Oeric (Oisc) and not from Hengest. Perhaps Hengest was not Oeric's father.

This allows us a lineage as follows: [Hengest, the first leader, dies in 467. I suggest Hengest was born C.390 and have elsewhere indicated what is potentially a piece of his background.]

The Royal Dynasty of Kent

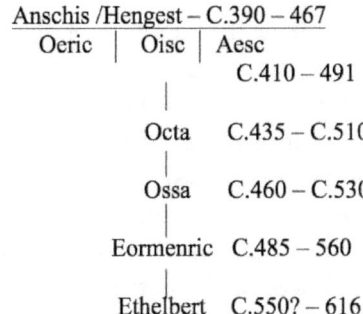

```
Anschis /Hengest – C.390 – 467
  Oeric  |  Oisc  |  Aesc
                     C.410 – 491
                     |
              Octa   C.435 – C.510
              |
              Ossa   C.460 – C.530
              |
         Eormenric   C.485 – 560
              |
         Ethelbert   C.550? – 616
```

The Historia Brittonum account of Arthur is clear that his principal (Kentish) opponent was Octa. In fact one can doubt the compiler's believing that Arthur had any non-Kentish enemies.

Regardless of the bloodline, perhaps all Englishmen, but definitely the inhabitants of Kent, were derisively referred to as Long-tails in the middle ages, at least till the 17th century and especially by the French according to the scholar John Ray. This may have been because of their supposed descents from horses. However, a very early witness, the Ravenna Cosmographer, about the time of Bede, calls the Saxon leader, Anschis. (I lately found a record of a Saxon named Anschitz, who was imprisoned in the Bastille in the early 18th century.)

I would make the suggestion that a warrior named Anschis carried the similar-sounding nickname Hengest, just as Oeric was called Aesc or Oisc. One might add, that Hengest's brother's name might have been entirely displaced by his nickname based on Anschis' own. But Horsa appears to have been a real Saxon name, so Hengest might have become a nickname because of his brother Horsa's real name.

Again, it may be worth considering whether the traditional distinctions of 'Man of Kent' and 'Kentishman' have their origins in the uneasy relationship which the

Kent rulers and their followers had with their British subjects, geographical division being perhaps created. I have no idea if such a theory holds water. The Historia Brittonum has no awareness of Oeric and believes Octa Hengest's son. Isn't it possible or even probable that when, according to the Historia Brittonum, Octa came down from the north (and from land held beside Hadrian's Wall) it was while Octa's true father Oeric, now no longer young, was still alive?

Octa had perhaps fought the Britons (and Arthur) in the north. Now (467 - 479) was the lead-up to Mount Badon. Octa appears to have been an important figure, whose significance is apparently preserved in placenames such as Otford and Otham. He may not have died in the subsequent fighting but lived out an inglorious reign after Oeric's death. He was probably the leader of the vanquished at Mount Badon.[*] Nothing is known of the subsequent Kent kings, his son and grandson, Ossa and Eormenric, except for their names.[†]

---

[*] But Osla Big Knife is named as Arthur's opponent at Mount Badon, in *The Dream of Rhonabwy*.

[†] Bede knows nothing of Ossa and believes Octa the father of Eormenric.

FAMILIES OF VORTIGERN AND AMBROSIUS

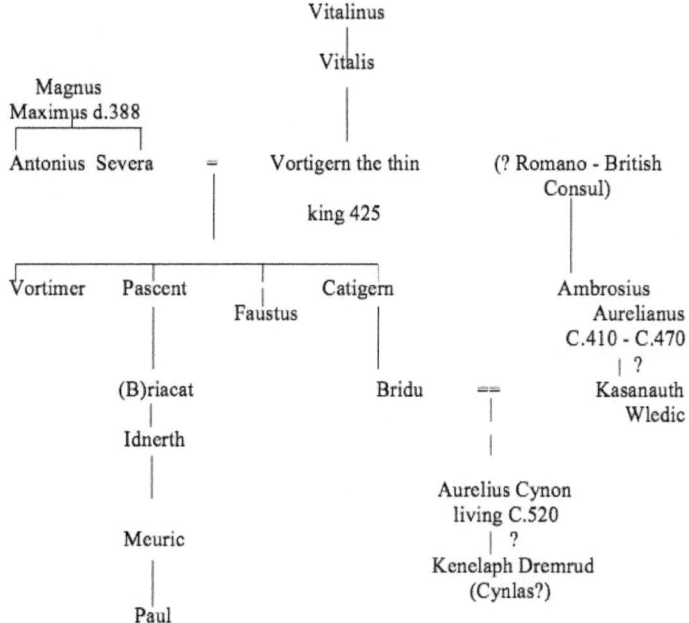

I suggest here that Kasanauth is son of Ambrosius: he bears the title Wledic[27] like his father. Aurelius Cynon, Gildas' king, could therefore be his son, for Aurelius is named obscurely by Gildas as Ambrosius' grandson. Cynon's son Kenelaph Dremrud, whether or not Cuneglas (Cynlas), has the red face (dremrud) that might suggest a descent from Ambrosius.[*]

---

[*] Ambrosius is called *guletic* in a story recorded in the Historia Brittonum. Cynon is named as a son of Kasanauth in the genealogies. I do not wish to deny the possibility that *dremrud* refers to a high colour and not to blushing. If Kenelaph were Cuneglas (one of the kings attacked by Gildas),

it is odd that Gildas does not refer to his father or ancestry, and seems to indicate Aurelius Cynon as Ambrosius' family's solitary survivor. Another Cynlas is indicated by the genealogies as son of Eugen (Danwyn) and therefore cousin of Maelgwn. But Maelgwn destroyed Eugen. So he is less likely to have been king. I believe that Kasanauth's marriage to Pascent's niece would be further evidence of goodwill between the families (see p.52)

ROYAL DUMNONIAN GENEALOGY

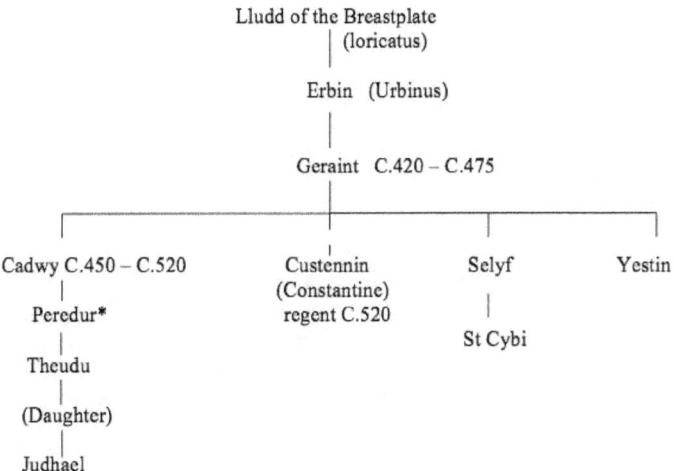

---

* If Peredur lived long enough to have children, C.520 he might have been dead and it was *his* sons murdered by Constantine. He was surely too old to have been one of Constantine's victims.

THE DESCENTS FROM CUNEDDA: ARTHUR'S FAMILY

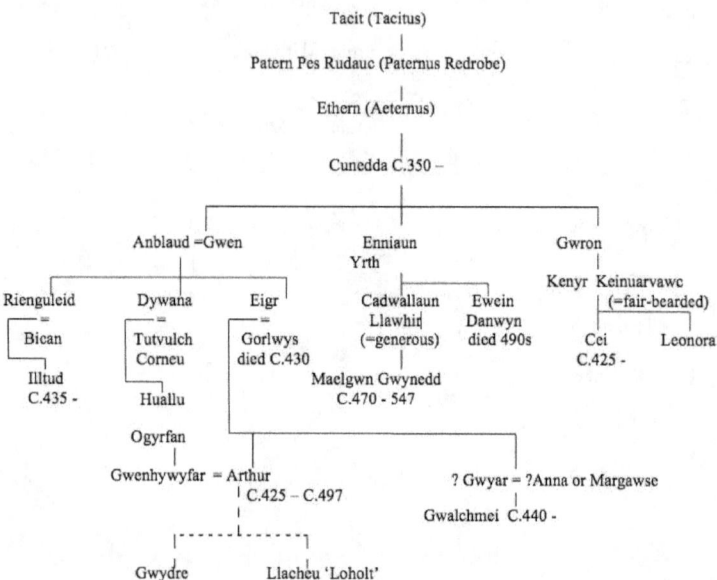

Eigr has a brother named in *Culhwch and Olwen* as Gorfoddw. Perhaps her husband *Gor*lwys is also her cousin.

MAPS

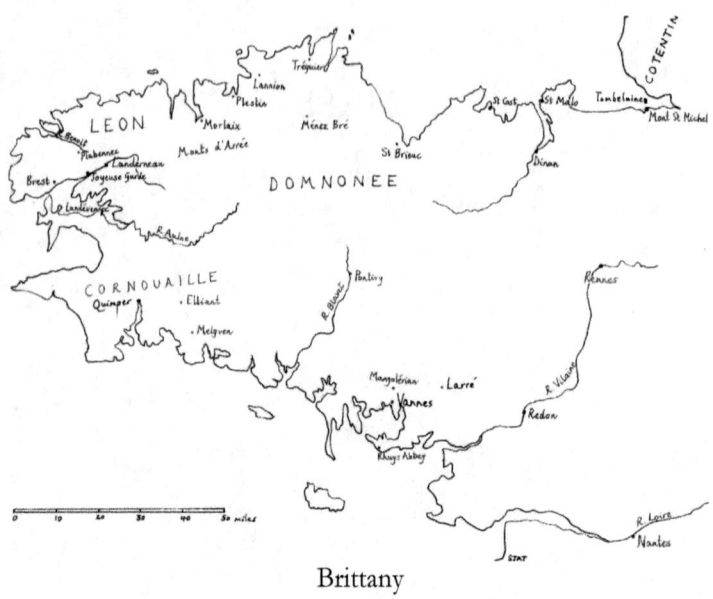

Brittany

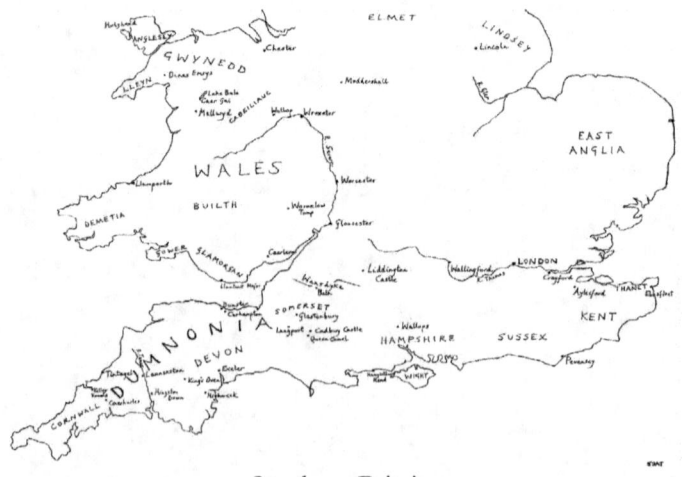

Southern Britain

Maps | 217

Northern Britain

A SUMMARY LIFE OF ARTHUR

c.425	Born in Tintagel, Cornwall (W. Dumnonia) to a local chieftain Gorlwys and his wife, Eigr, a princess.
c.430	Fostered out to Eigr's 1st cousin, Kenyr living beside Bala Lake in mid-Wales. Arthur becomes friendly with Kenyr's son, Cei, and a local boy, Bedwyr, son of Bedrawc.
Late 430s	Goes to Quimper in Brittany - for education?
440s	Falls in love with Cei's sister Leonora. First military experience. Plays a part in a victory over the Frankish King Chlodio outside Paris.
450s - 464	Involved in joint actions with the Roman military commander Aegidius. Marries Gwenhwyfar.
c.465 - c.479	In Britain, mainly fighting in the North. Has a main hand in completing the resistance work initiated by Ambrosius.
c.479	Defeats the Saxons at Mount Badon.
c.480 - c.497	Living peacefully in Dumnonia ruled by his friend, the young king Cadwy.

c.497   Following a disastrous altercation involving Gwenhwyfar, dies fighting Medraut, the aristocratic grandson of an old friend, at Camlan. He leaves behind not only his wife but his devoted mistress Garwen. His burial-place is a mystery.

Sources For Arthur And His Circle, As Found In The Main Text

Cap 1   *Arthur's own good friend …*

             See Appendix 1; the Life of Carantoc is the principal reason for this belief.

Cap 2   Birth and Parentage …. See Geoffrey's History VIII.

             Anblaud … See e.g. The Life of Illtud.

             Igerna's (second?) husband … See *Culhwch and Olwen*.

Cap 3   Kenyr as foster-father… This is a deduction from Kay's father Ector being Arthur's foster-father (in Malory).

             Two early poets … i.e. William Llŷn and Ieuan Brydydd Hir.

             Triad on Kenyr … See note for reference.

             Ector … See Malory 1.

             Leonora … See H.O. Summer - Vulgate Cycle II. 124 & III. 159.

Rienguleid and Bican ... See The Life of Illtud.

Sefin ... Cei's father ... See the dialogue poem between Melvas and Gwenhwyfar mentioned in Supplementary Note 18.

Cap 7   *Arthur's cousin Illtud* ... See reference in note.

Cap 8   Arthur in Gaul ... the references are to William the Chaplain's Life of Goueznou (1019) and to Geoffrey IX as stated.

Arthur and Flollo ... See Geoffrey IX.

Cap 9   Arthur and Aegidius ... See references to authors in text.

Arthur and Lucius Hiberius ... See Geoffrey IX.

Cap 10   Ogyrfan and Gwenhwyfar ... See e.g. Siôn Cent.

Cap 11   Gwalchmei ... See William of Malmesbury's Historia III.

A very early Welsh poem ... Tryfrwyd ... See Black Book of Carmarthen XXXI.

Cap 14 ... *an old Welsh poem on the death of Geraint* ... See the poem on Llongborth in the Black Book of Carmarthen.

Abbot Wrdisten ... refers to him ... See The Life of Winwaloe.

And in another saint's life ... See The Life of Carantoc.

One is Ligessauc Llawhir ... See The Life of Cadoc.

But in earlier literature he [Hueil] stabs Gwydre ... See *Culhwch and Olwen*.

Cap 15 *One follower of Arthur's ... Lancelot* ... See Malory passim.

Cap 16 *Loholt was said to be their son, and elsewhere Borre* ... See details on Leonora (cap. 3), and Malory I for Borre.

Ogyrfan whom Arthur is said ... to have aided against King Ryons ... See Malory 1

Ogyrfan's son ... Yvain of Cavaliot ... See note in text but also R. Bromwich (ed.) - Trioedd Ynys Prydein pp. CXIV - CXV for another explanation.

[Caradawc] *is associated in Welsh tradition with ... Glamorgan* ... See Jesus College Mss Gen. IX.

[Llacheu's] *death ... supposed to have happened 'below Llech Ysgar'* ... See Bleddyn Fardd.

Brastias ... See Malory 1: he is a knight of Uther's before following Arthur.

Ewein ... the son of king Uriens of Gore ... See Malory 1.

[Illtud] *headed for the court of his cousin* ... See The Life of Illtud.

Arthur is recorded as having a court in Cornwall at ... Celli Wig ... See e.g. *Culhwch and Olwen* and Triad 1. (Mike Ashley would dispute the court was in Cornwall and search in Wales, where a Celli Wig still exists.)

Morgana ... Margawse ... Elaine ... See e.g. Malory 1.

Cap 17 *Medraut ... grandson of ... Caradawc Strong Arm and son of one of the holy men of the period* ... See

A.W. Wade-Evans - Vitae Sanctorum Britanniae, 322, 51.

There is a story of Melvas ... See Caradoc's Life of Gildas.

Cap 18 *Morfran son of Tegid is one* ... See *Culhwch and Olwen*.

Osfran's son was buried at Camlan ... See The Song of the Graves in the Black Book of Carmarthen.

Bedwyr ... buried on Tryvan ... Ditto as above.

Spear ... in 1535 ... described ... according to the parish rector ... See S. Baring-Gould and J.Fisher - Lives of the British Saints, IV. 103.

William ... tells us ... See reference above to Cap 11.

In an early Welsh poem Gwalchmei ... buried ... Monnow ... See Sir Ifor Williams' note in his edition of the Prophecy of Britain (Armes Prydein). The poem is The Song of the Graves (Black Book of Carmarthen).

A more modern source ... See Lewis Morris - Celtic Remains P.213.

> *There is no mention of Arthur's sword* ... See
> Benedict of Peterburgh's Acts of King Richard.

Cap 19 *In the story of Hueil* ... See Caradoc's Life of
> Gildas.

> *These are the words he spoke to a certain Cribwr* ...
> See 16th cent. Text on the Giants in Pen. 118.

> [Drudwas] *is said to have had a sister, Erdudfyl, who
> was Arthur's mistress* ... See *Culhwch and Olwen*.

> *One ... fantasy includes her but another ... version
> does not* ... See Mss Mostyn 146 and Robert
> Vaughan's 1655 letter to M. Lloyd.

> *An old stanza* ... See Trioedd Ynys Prydein
> P.354.

> *Arthur's own land* ... See Hermann of Tournai's
> Miracles of St Mary of Laon II. 15 (C. 1146).

To reiterate what I have stated elsewhere, I have stopped short of claiming in this work *absolute proof* of any aspect of Arthur's life - however I may have expressed myself at times as if such-and-such relative to Arthur were to be treated as a fact. This is because of the lack of contemporary documentation of Arthur's existence.

However, in such details as the fostering out of Arthur to the family of Kenyr *with the unnoticed genealogical connexion between Eigr and Kenyr*, it seems to me *overwhelmingly likely* that we are touching upon historical reality.

And, for instance, I would say the same about Camlan, though the attendant detail is more confusing. Nor do I question Arthur's leadership in the resistance (as in the ancient poem on Llongborth), leading up to the Badon siege, a conclusive battle in the year of Gildas' birth and one attributed to Arthur by Nennius and the Annales Cambriae. It is hard to see how it could have been fought by Ambrosius (fighting since 436), but there has even been an attempt to propose an Ambrose junior. What can one say?

This still leaves a question mark over whether all the battles in the battle-list were won by Arthur, and likewise over the lengthy period that I suggest he spent in Brittany (though for my part I feel a certain confidence in his love affair or marriage with Kenyr's daughter at Quimper).

There *are* negative arguments against Arthur's existence, and I have tried to include something of these: Taliesin's battle of the Cells of Brewyn 'long celebrated', fought (one would suppose) by his patron Urien of Rheged was an opportunity to mention Arthur, but the mention did not occur; the author of *Armes Prydein*, the Prophecy of Britain, likewise declined to include Arthur; Gildas also disappoints, though the omission here may be in line with mediaeval ecclesiastical opinion that Arthur, whatever his military prowess, was a scoundrel.

I ask in the end that the reader make up his or her own mind on the basis of the evidence I have given, applying some private version of the laws of probability. I hope the historical Arthur will emerge triumphant from this process.

Obviously, the presence of a still greater man, the Romano-British Ambrosius Aurelianus, in the same period clouds the issue. But this is no reason to deny Arthur his due.

GLOSSARY

Avalon - It is to the island of Avalon that Arthur is sent for healing after Camlan. In Malory, it is the Vale of Avilion. Avalon, apparently from a Celtic rootword for apple, has been identified with Glastonbury in Somerset (eastern Dumnonia), within a famous apple-growing region. The cross found in Arthur's supposed grave bore an inscription pointing to this identification. The island of Aiguillon off Brittany was also linked with Arthur.* The Bretons had ancient stories of nine wise women, virgin priestesses reminiscent of Arthur's female attendants and inhabiting the island of Sena. The original Avalon was probably an Otherworld and, in Geoffrey's Life of Merlin, it is also named The Fortunate Island. Here, his labours done, Arthur came for an enduring peace.

Dumnonia - The south-western kingdom of the Britons, whose name is preserved in modern Devon, supposedly from root-words meaning 'the deep valleys'. Originally extending, from west to east, over Cornwall, Devon and much of Somerset, it had shrunk by the middle of the 8th century to simply Cornwall guarded by the river Tamar. There is a letter surviving from Aldhelm, the early 8th century English bishop of Sherborne, to King Geraint. Cornwall fell to the English in the 9th century. About 930, King Athelstan expelled the British from Exeter, where they had their own quarter as a flourishing enclave.

---

* North-west of Morlaix, off the coast by Perroz-Guirec where Arthur is said to have held his court, 'the Bretons say [he] was buried in the islet of Agalon.' (Black's Brittany and Touraine, 1905). Augustus Hare also records the burial tradition in the 1890s. It is not clear how old it is. The island is in private hands. It is now called Aval.

The Cornish maintained a remarkable separateness, and, till the 18th century, even their own language, though this was only in western pockets. A few works of Cornish literature survive, but not pre-mediaeval. It is no wonder if Cornwall, the land of Tintagel and the lost Celliwig, is replete with Arthurian legends and traditions; and if the rest of Dumnonia to the east that includes Glastonbury and Cadbury Castle has its own share of Celtic stories.

Excalibur - Arthur's sword, distinct from the one he extracts from the stone to become king, is called Caliburn by Geoffrey who says it was forged in Avalon. It is the Caledvwlch or Caladbolg borrowed from the Irish hero Cuchulainn.

Federates - Those bound by a treaty (Latin 'foedus').

Genealogies - While (like the Triads) they are not renowned for their reliability, some give evidence of great antiquity, and they remain a precious historical resource, sometimes tracing important Celtic families back to Roman beginnings. There is no good reason to support Sir Edmund Chambers when he declares those relating to Arthur are all mediaeval concoctions.

Historia Britannica - Did Geoffrey really have a Breton history on which he drew extensively, on which the author of the life of Goueznou also drew in 1019 when he perhaps refers to it? I believe such a compilation from the 9th or 10th century did exist, and that, for instance, Geoffrey may have taken Flollo's name from it (see Cap.8). On this intriguing subject see further 'The Arthur of the Welsh ed. R. Bromwich et al., 1991, pp. 265-6. Rachel Bromwich also states that 'it is evident that

Geoffrey derived his form of the name [of Medraut] from a Cornish or Breton source.' We must not forget that, if there had been a Breton version of the Historia Brittonum, it might have incorporated Breton additions. Such a work *could have been* the Historia Britannica.

Historia Brittonum - This compilation is from a variety of sources which the last compiler (Nennius), building on the work of others, has in his own words 'heaped together'. He wrote C.830, but in its earliest form it might be 7th century or even earlier. The materials are of varying significance, but the Historia Brittonum is a precious resource. Its relationship with the unproven Historia Britannica (seemingly, a Breton history of the Britons covering some of the same later ground) is an important field for speculation. I have used the term 'the compiler' in the text, not 'Nennius', because the entries were clearly made at different times. However where it is clearly *the last compiler*, I call him this - or Nennius.

The Holy Grail - This first makes its appearance in the 12th century work of Chrétien de Troyes, one of the greatest romance writers. While there may be a pagan origin in some Celtic vessel, it is generally associated by early writers with Christianity. The mystery and wonder it brought to Arthurian tales was a main factor in their popularity.

Merlin - There is no space to touch more than very briefly on the involved question of this British prophetic bard. He seems to have been largely an invention of Geoffrey's. The British, and Geoffrey himself, loved prophecy. Merlin's name is linked by Geoffrey with Carmarthen, Caermyrddin, where he first makes an appearance in

Geoffrey's work. His prophetic activities probably owe much to a legend in which Ambrosius meets Vortigern and tells him the future; and a series of stories based around a strange Scotsman called Lailocen from the end of the 6th century. Geoffrey's accounts of Merlin vary hugely between his History and his later work The Life of Merlin so that the received wisdom, first finding expression in Giraldus, became that there were two Merlins - Merlin Ambrosius and Merlin of the Forest. Myrddin might truly have existed under his own name, but he does not figure in the Historia Brittonum list of bards, and he certainly had nothing to do with Arthur.

Romances - The tales of Arthur by which he is best known. With the exception of the primitive *Culhwch and Olwen* our surviving texts begin in date after Geoffrey and continue to C.1500. They are to be used with utmost caution for any historical content. See the Preface for some early material in Malory whose work stands at the culmination and - more or less - conclusion of the Romantic tradition.

The Round Table - The table appears to have been lifted from Irish legend. It is first clearly found in the 12th century Brut of the Jersey-born Norman Wace. A Welsh poem gives Arthur a long table but does not call it round.

Saxons - This was the name generally used by the Britons for the Germanic invaders. I have retained it, though 'English' would be more accurate. These Germans were especially Angles, Saxons and Jutes. Hengest may have been a Jute. See Bede's work for further details. Compare the Scottish term 'Sassenach' for those from south of the border.

Triads - These groups of historical threesomes are of varying date, some truly ancient, and others belonging to the Middle Ages. Not easy to assess for their accuracy, they sometimes throw in precious detail of which we have no other trace.

Tristan - The romantic tale of the love of Tristan and Yseult concerns Dumnonia and Brittany. It is a 6th century story involving the wicked king Mark. Mark has been identified but not confidently with Cunomorus, Cynvawr of the royal Dumnonian family tree, and therefore closely related to the reprehensible Constantine. Breton folklore remembers Cynvawr as a prototype of the appalling Bluebeard,[*] serial killers of women both. An inscribed stone in Cornwall, near Fowey, once marking a burial site, bears Tristan's name.

Wealhas - The name given in the Anglo-Saxon Chronicle to the Britons after only the first two entries from the time of the Saxon arrival. Thereafter, the Britons began to be called the wealhas, the foreigners, now the Welsh. How much better their own term, the Combrogi, allies, now the Cymry. Until very recent times, a district south of the Scottish border was called Cumberland, now a portion of Cumbria.

---

[*] Gilles de Rais

SOME VARIANT NAMES

(M) - As found in Malory
(G) - As found in Geoffrey
(?) - Not necessarily the same person
Aesc, Oisc, Oeric
Aegidius, Gillon, Giles
Ambrosius, Embreis, Emrys
Angus, Anguissance (M), Angwas(?)
Bedwyr, Bedivere (M)
Bledhericus, Blaise (M)
Brastias (M), Briocatus (?)
Cadwy, Cador (M), Cato
Chlodio, Flollo (G)
Cian, Gwenc'hlan
Eigr, Igraine (M), Igerna (G)
Galahad (M), Gwalhafed (?)
Gorlwys, Gorlois (M)
Gwalchmei, Gawain (M), Gavin, Walwyn
Gwenhwyfar, Guinevere (M), Jennifer
Illtud, Eltut, Eliduc (?)
Kenyr, Sefin, Sevain (?), Sanam (?) (M), Ector (M) = ? Protector
Lancelot (M), Lanzelet, Launval (?)
Llacheu, Loholt (?) = ? Flaccus
Leonora, Lissanor, Eleanor, Lionors (M)
Medraut, Mordred (M), Modred
Ogyrfan, Leodegrance (M)

CHRONOLOGY

383-388 Magnus Maximus' rebellion
407-411 Constantine's rebellion
409-10 Saxon devastation in Britain
410 Sack of Rome by the Goths
410- The Britons fight back successfully. (A rescript from the emperor Honorius tells them to look after their own defences.) Hostility of Britons towards Romano-Britons
418 A traditional date for the departure of the Roman population from Britain
423 Death of Honorius
425 Aëtius active in Gaul. Valentinian III becomes emperor: he is six years old
Vortigern becomes paramount ruler of Britain. The last help from Gaul is received
c.425 Arthur is born in Tintagel, Cornwall, to Dumnonian aristocrats
428 Arrival of three keels with Hengest at Ypwinesfleot. The occupants are made federates and given Thanet, an island off Kent
429 The Hallelujah victory under Germanus is a defeat for a combined force of Saxons and Picts
c.430 Arthur's father dies. His mother remarries soon after. He is adopted by her first cousin and goes to live in Wales
434- Hengest breaks out. Battles with Vortimer
435- Germanus takes on a diplomatic role in Gaul, especially for the Armoricans
435 Battle of Crayford drives Britons out of Kent and into London
436 Battle of Guolopp(um), marking a rift between Vortigern's and Ambrosius' factions

c. 436	Massacre of Vortigern's Concilium
436/7	Revolt of the Bacaudae and Armoricans. Their leader Tibatto is captured and killed with the help of Hunnish mercenaries
c.440	Aetius defeats Chlodio and the Franks at Vicus Helena
440s	The Alans are sent by Aëtius against the Armoricans. Germanus tries to intercede. Success comes after his death. Arthur is in Quimper where he has an affair with Cei's sister. He takes part in a battle near Paris where Chlodio is defeated
c.444	Battle of Wippedsfleot
446	Britons appeal to Aetius for help: none comes
c.450s	Arthur in Britain where he falls in love with and marries Guinevere
451	The Hunnish invasion of Gaul culminates in the battle of the Catalaunian Plain, in which Aetius, with Gothic and Breton help, stops Attila's advance
452?	Devastation of Armorica by Goths, Frisians and Saxons
452	The great Western raid sees Hengest's army reach as far as south-western coastland, probably Dumnonian
c.453	Ambrosius fights back successfully, though many Britons are fleeing abroad. Other British successes follow
454/55	Murder of Aetius by Valentinian. Murder of Valentinian some months later
456	Childeric, king of the Franks, is expelled by his people, who invite Aegidius, supreme commander in Gaul, to be their leader
457	Majorian becomes emperor

CHRONOLOGY | 235

460s	Aegidius, with Frankish (and Breton?) help, drives the Alans and Visigoths back to the Loire. He also besieges Chinon, in unknown circumstances
461	Murder of Majorian by Ricimer. He is replaced by Libius Severus. Aegidius independent of Roman authority, ruling from Soissons
463/4	Childeric returns to power. He and Aegidius (and Bretons?) defeat the Goths at Orléans. Childeric abandons his allegiance and fights Aegidius between Laon and Rheims
464	Death of Aegidius by foul play. Syagrius succeeds him as ruler of the Soissons "kingdom"
465	Beginning of blockade of Paris by the Franks
c.465	Return of Arthur to Britain? British victories follow
467	Hengest dies; his son Aesc rules in Kent
469	The emperor Anthemius requests British help against the Visigoths. King Riothamus comes with 12,000 men; in a protracted battle he is defeated at Déols before he can link with a Roman force; he flees into Burgundy; while there, bishop Sidonius writes him a letter, the text still surviving
471 -	Further British success under Arthur culminating in ....
479	... the siege of Mount Badon. The end of the serious fighting. The Arthurian Peace. Gildas is born
475	End of the blockade of Paris
476	Romulus Augustulus, last emperor, is deposed - a symbolic moment for the fall of the western empire
481	Clovis succeeds his father Childeric

485	The battle of Mearcraedesburn, probably in Sussex and indecisive. An agreement is reached with Aelle, king of the South Saxons
486	Clovis defeats Syagrius at Soissons. Syagrius is put to death
491	Massacre of the inhabitants of Pevensey Castle by the South Saxons; death of Aesc. Clovis chases Bretons out of region between Tours and Orléans
496/7	The Franks, unable to defeat the Bretons, make a treaty. Among the conditions, the Bretons recognize Frankish supremacy and are disallowed kings of their own; and Clovis must become Christian
497	Battle of Camlan; Medraut dies, Arthur also or mortally wounded
500-	Eusebius "king of Vannes" puts down a revolt at Comblessac
c.520	Cadwy king of Dumnonia dies; Constantine is made regent and murders Cadwy's sons; Gildas writes his "De Excidio"
547	Maelgwn of North Wales dies of the Yellow Plague. Following this devastation, the Saxons renew their campaigning against the Britons
570	Death of Gildas
590s	A British defeat is the subject of a long poem, still preserved, by the bard Aneirin, the earliest writer to mention Arthur

FURTHER READING

The Anglo-Saxon Chronicle (trans. G.N Garmonsway) Dent, 1967.

Ashley, Mike - *The Mammoth Book of King Arthur* - Robinson, 2005.

Bromwich, R & others (ed.) - *The Arthur of the Welsh* - Univ. of Wales, 1991.

Bromwich, R (ed.) - *Trioedd Ynys Prydein* - Univ. of Wales, 1961.

Chambers, Sir E.K - *Arthur of Britain* - Speculum Historiale, 1964.

Coe, J.B & Young, S - *The Celtic Sources for the Arthurian Legend* - Llanerch, 1995.

Fleuriot, Léon - *Les origines de la Bretagne* - Payot & Rivages, 1999.

Genealogies and Texts (Arthurian Sources Vol V) (Prepared by J Morris) - Phillimore, 1995.

Gildas - *The Ruin of Britain (Arthurian Sources Vol VII)* (trans. M. Winterbotham) - Phillimore, 2002.

La Villemarqué, Théodore Hersart de - *Le Barzaz Breizh* - Coop Breizh, 1997.

Loomis - R.S (ed.) - *Arthurian Literature in the Middle Ages* - Clarendon, 1969.

Malory, Sir T. - *Works* (ed. E. Vinaver) - O.U.P, 1971.

Monmouth, Geoffrey of - *The History of the Kings of Britain* (trans. L. Thorpe) - Penguin, 1966.

Morris, John - *The Age of Arthur* - Sutton, 1998.

Nennius - *British History (Arthurian Sources Vol VIII)* (trans. John Morris) - Phillimore, 1980.

Snyder, C.A - *An Age of Tyrants* - Weidenfeld & Nicolson, 1989.

White, R. (ed.) - *King Arthur in Legend and History* - Dent, 1997.

GENERAL ACKNOWLEDGEMENTS

Temporarily without access to the great libraries, I owe principal debts to authors of works in my own, on certain of whom I have leaned heavily. I should particularly like to mention Rachel Bromwich, doyenne of Celtic scholars, Léon Fleuriot, Roger Sherman Loomis, and John Morris, not now all amongst the living. I wish to thank John Walcot for his friendly interest; Stephen Terry for many useful suggestions and his map work; Jo Druett who has had to make sense of my handwriting; Roger Collicott for tracking down elusive texts; Wayne Travis and Robyn Bromfield for their photographic skills; and the late and honoured James Tilly whose photography adorns the front cover. My task would have been very much harder or impossible without all of these.

ACKNOWLEDGEMENTS TO TRANSLATORS

The passages in translation quoted in the main text are from:

M.Winterbotham - Gildas

J. Morris - Historia Brittonum

G.N. Garmonsway - The Anglo-Saxon Chronicle

R. Bromwich - Trioedd Ynys Prydein (Not only the Triads, but much else)

Lewis Thorpe - Gregory of Tours

A.W. Wade-Evans - The Life of Illtud

R. White - Gerald of Wales and others

W.W. Comfort - Chrétien de Troyes

Meirion Pennar - Taliesin

J.B. Coe and S. Young - Teyrnon's Chair and other texts

Jack Lindsay - Gallic Chronicles

Geoffrey Ashe - Late French Chronicles

C.D. Gordon - John of Antioch and Priscus

In a few cases I have slightly adapted the translations, and, in a few cases, the translations are my own. The remaining translations are also my own. I apologize in advance if any translator has not been acknowledged, owing my thanks to all of these, whose publishers' permission has been sought for my use of their quotations.

Supplementary Notes

1) I wonder whether it is worth looking at Gildas' possible debt to Dares of Phrygia's de Excidio Troiae, Downfall of Troy. (There was also a Greek version by Tryphiodorus)[*]. In a nod to this work, Gildas might have seen the Saxons *invited in* by Vortigern as the Britons' Trojan Horse. But there is nothing explicit in Gildas' text. 'Wolves into the sheepfold' is his closest utterance.

I note here also Joseph of Exeter's comment in his 12th century 'Trojan War': 'So in their absurd faith and naïve error the Britons await Arthur … and will wait for ever.' (III. 472-3)

2) It is possible that one of those 'who could not be expelled (?) from Arthur's Court', Uchei son of Gwryon,[†] is Cei's uncle, brother of Kenyr. This involves identifying Kenyr's father Gwron with Gwryon. Uchei son of Gwryon is also recorded as Etheu son of Gwrgon. Such an identification would explain his privileged status. I do not believe that *Culfanawyd* son of Gwryon (*Culhwch and Olwen*) or *Cadwri* son of Gwrion (*Geraint son of Erbin*) clarify this issue at all. (*Cadwri* might be king Cadwy, and therefore his father 'Gwrion' an error for Geraint).

3) From an early date, Vortigern had the reputation of having usurped power; perhaps this is even implied by Gildas' calling him *tyrannus*, tyrant, though *superbus*

---

[*] There are passages in this author after L.575 reminiscent of Gildas cap. 24.

[†] Triad 74.

tyrannus, proud tyrant, might be a loose adaptation of his position as *overlord* or even of his name/title. (Vortigern = Great Lord, in Brythonic). In the life of Goueznou (1019), he is a usurper; and Geoffrey also presents him thus. We do not know the basis for this belief, but the negative feelings attached to him for his role in the coming of the Saxons may help account for it. He is recorded as being of an obviously distinguished family in the area of Gloucestershire, a region loved by the Romans and was presumably a local chieftain. Is it not possible that his rise to paramount sovereign in 425 came on the back of the Romans' suggesting to the Britons a supreme leader and giving him their backing for the nomination?

4) Vortigern's mother-in-law, whose daughter Severa he married, was a deeply pious woman. A charming chapter of Sulpicius Severus' Life of Saint Martin tells us how she, an empress, waited upon St Martin at table, in pure reverence. Following Theophanes, we may note Severa as a relative of the short-lived emperor Maximus (455).

5) Chlodio's second successor Childeric apparently figures later in Geoffrey's text as a Saxon invader of Britain, Cheldric. This may be a composite name, combining the Merovingian king with another invader, recorded in the A-S Chronicle, Cerdic. Lewis Carroll hardly did better when he created *Rilchiam* from Richard and William. (Lucius Hiberius of whom more elsewhere may be another such composite name.) It is the *form* of Flollo's name, not understood by Geoffrey, that is so intriguing.

6) 'The land of the Picts' may be a reference to Galloway, for a number of early English writers refer to Galloway in this way, however mistakenly. These include Reginald of Durham, Jocelin of Furness, Richard and John of

Hexham. For instance, Reginald in a book on Saint Cuthbert places Kirkudbright *in terra Pictorum*; Jocelin mentions *Pictorum patriam*, the Picts' homeland, *que modo Galwiethia dicitur*, now called Galloway. These writers are not much after Lambert and may be a clue to a general confusion. But Galloway, misdescribed or not, may be the most likely site for the palace.

About the time of the 1st world war, it is said that two brothers on a remote Galloway farm discovered a golden statue of a god 7 feet high in a peat bog, perhaps the last place of concealment of the Picts' greatest treasure, though it might be British. The man who recorded this story held the last golden fist in his own hand for all else had been dismembered and sold to a local bullion merchant.

7) I further note that Mynydd Amanw, in *Culhwch and Olwen*, might be Mount Damen. In *The Dream of Rhonabwy* figures the character with the odd name of Daned son of Oth: could this be a grave memorial recording that a son of Oth (i.e Octa) died at the battle of [Mount] Agned (= Daned?) However, I have recently found two Breton placenames, Kerdanet or Kerdaned, one near Roscoff and the other at Pleyben Le -Cloître.

8) Ronald Millar has managed to find locations for all the battle-list in Brittany! The best of these seem to be:
The river *Daoulas*, near Brest, in *Léon*.
Castel *Guennon* at Tregon, near Dinard.
The river Trieaux (formerly *Trifrouit*) at Lanleff.
Ste Anne (formerly Ste *Agned*) near the village of *Brech*.
Baden, near Vannes, on the Gulfe du Morbihan.

I do not know whether the last two are hills. Vannes was the legionary capital of Armorica, but I doubt it was ever called the City of the Legion, as Millar suggests. In passing, I might mention that Arthur's legendary seat, Carduel *can* be found in Brittany near Trozoul. He is also said to have founded the Château at Auray destroyed in 1558.

9) The delightful and whimsical mediaeval tale found in the Mabinogion, *The Dream of Rhonabwy*, presents its own curious version of the lead-up to Badon, where the enemy is named as Osla Big-knife. The site of the battle is in Welsh Montgomeryshire (now part of Powys) close to Fordun. Nearby is Rhyd-y-groes, the Ford of the Cross.

10) An intriguing passage in Ussher (P.254) gives a portion of a poem ascribed to Taliesin and translated into Latin by the 16th century Welsh historian Sir John Price: - O too wretched were those (madmen?) at the battle of Badon whose gore stained the sword of Arthur, leader of chieftains [benn haelion]* now avenging the blood spilt of heroes by whose aid the Northern Kingdoms survived (as was right) for many years.

What makes it so interesting is that if we place many of Arthur's battles from the battle-list in the north as there are grounds for doing, we are bemused to find an early Welsh poet who has anticipated us about fighting in the north. He seems to say that Badon was Arthur's means of vengeance upon those who had harried the northern kingdoms. This idea may be simply stolen from the Historia Brittonum which states Arthur's fighting in Britain began after Octa, the Kentishman, returned from his northern campaigning. But the author may be

---

* benn haelion is translated as *principis magnatum*. The expression reminds one of *the Lords of Emrys* i.e. Ambrosius was leader of the lords as Arthur was of the *haelion*.

distinguishing the last action, Badon, from the others, out of his own knowledge.

There is no claim made here that Arthur fought in the northern battles. The learned Price's expression *sub monte Badonis* i.e. below Mount Badon, not 'at the battle of Badon', may indicate his belief of a defending force defeating its besiegers. Such western sites as Bath - recorded in the Mirabilia as *Badon(is)* - might then be considered. The northern kingdoms would be Rheged and Elmet; Strathclyde survived much longer than these, though, if we place credence in Gwalchmei's expulsion from Galloway, with altered boundaries.

11) In his castigation of Aurelius Cynon (= Caninus), the grandson of Ambrosius Aurelianus, Gildas reminds him of the *supervacua phantasia*,* the utterly fanciful dream, of his fathers and brothers, all of whom are said to have died prematurely. I suggest this was a political fantasy originally derived from Ambrosius himself. It is of course anybody's guess what this could have been, but, given the large-scale nature of it,† might I propose it was the vast aspiration to create a northern coalition of kingdoms based on Britain and France? This might really have seemed possible in the mid years of the 5th century.‡ It is a shame that the term 'fathers' is so obscure: does Gildas think of Aurelius' father - and stepfather (if he had one)? Or perhaps he

---

* Michael Winterbotham's translation of this expression seems unlikely, and at variance with Gildas' other use of *phantasia*. (See De Excidio Cap.34 for Gildas' reference to Maelgwn's *dream* of rule by force.)

† It was also plainly common knowledge.

‡ Particularly after Majorian's death in 461 when the strength in the north coincided with the barbarian Ricimer's control southward.

means Aurelius' father and grandfather Ambrosius and even great grandfather: only the last is definitely recorded (by Gildas) as dying by violence. At any rate it would be an unusual way of referring to Aurelius' parents. (I hesitantly suggest that Gildas was once a supporter of the aspiration before cynicism set in, if we see behind *supervacua* a deep contempt.)

12) The text actually translates as 'we *desirably* desire' indicating a lack of fluency with Latin. *Fathers* may be better translated as *elders*.

13) The extremely interesting question of how such a text would be transmitted to the general population is unanswerable. The text may have been written in Brythonic also; interpreters, especially clerics, may have been relied upon. Perhaps after all this text came from a polemic or letter, only intended for an educated readership.

However, St Patrick's letter to Coroticus' soldiers, of nearly the same date, reminds us both of our ignorance in these matters, and that the unlearned were expected to appreciate the letter's content. One may doubt there was much understanding of vulgar Latin in this period, except amongst the upper classes and educated. A few bilingual grave inscriptions exist in ogham (an Irish script) and in simple Latin, from the 5th century and later. There are also Latin inscriptions exclusively. But these tell us little about the general populace.

14) The translation 'rebel king' makes no sense, and in fact *rebellis* is also used elsewhere by Caradoc to mean *'warlike'*.

15) Kenneth Jackson states that '… the use of cavalry as an organised military tactic was unknown in general in Dark Age Britain …' But I find it hard to believe that the likes of Ambrosius and Arthur did not respond to suceesful Roman tactics in Gaul, especially after Ecdicius' astonishing rout of 4,000 Gothic infantry in the early 470s, with a force of only 18 men, even before the period when stirrups were in use.

Cabal is named as Arthur's dog in Mirabilia that form part of the Historia Brittonum: this may be his horse, since that is what the Latin *caballus* means.[*] In the ancient Triads of the Horses, figures such as Sadyrnin (Saturninus, and perhaps Illtud's brother) and Custennin (Constantine) are named as owners. Gildas' obscure reference to Cuneglas as 'rider of many' and 'driver of the chariot …' can only be mentioned hesitantly. There is also the poem on the battle of Llongborth in which cavalry play a principal role. Did Roman tactics really disappear so quickly? We know for instance that Bretons were wearing legionary kit sometime into the 6th century - quaintly anachronistic.[†] I feel that, with the mid-5th-century British resurgence, a cavalry force would have been a priority. *Perhaps the successful fight-back was based on it.* This idea has nothing to do with mediaeval romance. The abandonment of such an advantage does not make sense in the later 5th century.

16) Christopher Snyder indicates most historians' preference for a Coroticus ruling over Strathclyde 'because Patrick says he has dealings with the Picts' and

---

[*] I do not favour this theory; a large hunting dog called 'horse' looks like Arthur's humour. However folk tradition favours a horse.

[†] Procopius. We also have evidence of an early 6th century Breton legion stationed near Orléans. (Legio Bretonum)

because the unknown author of a table of contents in The Book of Armagh calls Coroticus king of Aloo i.e. the Strathclyde capital, Dumbarton.

But there was a king of Cardigan called Ceredic i.e. Coroticus about this time. Here is what the Life of Carantoc has to say: Saint Carantoc was son of Keredic son of Cunedda descended from Romans, Ethern (Aeternus?) and Patern Pes Rudauc (Paternus Redrobe) who appears to have been a senior Roman officer, and Tacit (Tacitus). Cunedda's eldest son Tipipaun evidently stayed behind and died, as ruler(?), in Manau Guotodin when Cunedda came south. The other sons of Cunedda, after Cunedda's death, shared their father's lands, bounded by the rivers Doubyr Driv (Dee) and Guoun (Gwaun)...'They held many regions in western Britain'. Ceredic held Cardigan. 'And after he had held it, the Scots [i.e. Irish] came and fought with them, and occupied all the regions'.

This is all reasonably circumstantial, and Carantoc though not Ceredic is also said to have had dealings with Patrick, however misdescribed the dealings may be. We cannot rule out that that this is the king whose soldiers Patrick wrote to, though they are named as allies of the Picts and Scots. Typipaun's family in the north might be an explanation for Arthur's sister's northern marriage, for they would be cousins.[*] The genealogy would be as follows:

---

[*] Maelgwn Gwynedd's son became King of the Picts, and still earlier, Daniel Dremrud, son of Iaun Reith, may have become a King in Scotland.

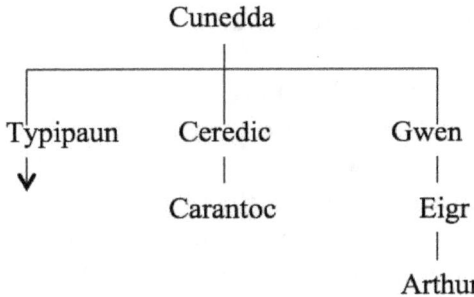

But a later date has been preferred for Carantoc - the 6th or 7th century - so uncertainty remains. In my chronology, Carantoc fits very neatly: he would probably be a few years older than Arthur; the cousins would both be beyond middle age at the time when they and Cadwy met if this event was post-Badon.

17) The Gwentian legal code, perhaps of the 12th century, bears witness to the fame of the Camlan story: when the queen desired a song in her chamber, the bard should sing the song of Camlan, but it was to be sung softly to prevent excitement in the hall. A king's reminder to his queen to remain faithful?

In the oral tradition, Gwenhwyfar had a bad reputation which also finds record in the Triads. Gwenhwy(f)ach appears to be an invented name based on Gwenhwyfar's and probably hides the name of Medraut, for reasons uncertain. Sir Ifor Williams proved that in one instance Gwenhwy(f)ach the name of Medraut.

18) Two old Welsh poems, apparently different versions of an encounter between Gwenhwyfar and Melvas and their subsequent conversation, in which Arthur is also involved, add little to our knowledge of the story. Melvas is taunted with his inferiority to Cei, and a previous meeting in Devon is referred to.

19) Deike Rich and Ean Begg describe this site of Camlan as follows: 'This feels a convincing place for a battle, a swampy valley, where a number of streams flow into the Afon Cerist. It lies beside the only way over the narrow, forbidding pass guarding the approaches to the harbours along Cardigan Bay.' (On the Trail of Merlin, Aquarian Press, 1991).

There is a story of Arthur dying at the hands (claws?) of Cath Paluc, the cat-monster. This looks like a variant on Camlan, but it is possible that Medraut had an ally. The obvious candidate is the young Maelgwn who would have been working on, or have succeeded in the absorption of Ewein Danwyn's kingdom into his own, and perhaps likewise Ogyrfan's kingdom of Cabeiliauc. Maelgwn's supposed fortress of Degannwy near Anglesey is recorded by Leland as Cerrig Gwinion; and Cei is said to have crossed to Anglesey apparently to kill the cat; another (French) story says the cat became king (of England) after killing Arthur - a storyteller for once bridging the gap between a monster and a potentially historical figure, since cats do not become kings.[*] Gildas

---

[*] Degannwy is situated on the east bank of the river Conway, on the mainland a little to the east of Anglesey, and was occupied in the period. Maelgwn may have been ruler of Anglesey: Gildas calls him 'dragon of the island'. Of course we are free to consider the cat-monster story as (Irish?) folklore like Twrch Trwyth; but cannot folklore grow out of or in combination with historical reality? The Anglesey connexion (as also in Triad 26) is interesting. Maelgwn's links with Anglesey are strong in tradition. These include St Eilian's church at Llaneilian on land granted by Maelgwn's father after Eilian had cured him (Cadwallaun) of blindness; and Ynys Seiriol (now Puffin Island), half a mile offshore where Maelgwn and his cousin Seiriol are said to lie buried, in the monastic cemetery: Seiriol, a monk and saint, used to meet St Cybi at Clorach; Cybi, another

also identifies humans with animals.

Perhaps Maelgwn is also the original of the Cheshire cat! Known by his contemporaries not for his smile but his enormous size, he is described by Gildas as remarkably generous - indeed Baring-Gould was appalled by Gildas' ingratitude for benefits he thought received by Gildas' family - and also as surrounded by sycophantic bards singing his praises.

Less pleasing is the story of how he killed his first wife and nephew to enjoy in peace the company of his nephew's wife who colluded in and encouraged his plan. (All this after he had made a stab at becoming a monk!) A remarkable man then, but his involvement in Camlan is quite uncertain, though feasible by date and politics. Gildas records his killing many chieftains (*tyranni*) and expelling others from their territory but names none, though obviously Ewein Danwyn was amongst these. Maelgwn became, within a few years of Arthur's death, or even immediately, very likely the most powerful Briton of his time, so that his death C.547 at the end of a long reign over Gwynedd (much of North Wales) became a well-remembered event. Cerdic, the continental Briton, was beginning to establish his Wessex kingdom but was effectively a foreign invader like Hengest.

It is important to remember the animal nature of so many names in the 5th century: Cynlas (Grey Dog), Gwalchmei (Hawk of the Plain?), and perhaps Arthur himself (Arth = Bear); the unimportant Turquin killed by Lancelot, in Malory, looks very like Twrch(g)wyn i.e. White Boar.

---

recipient of land from Maelgwn, established a monastery at Caergybi (Holyhead). St Deiniol, a further alleged beneficiary, being given land at nearby Bangor on the mainland, had a son commemorated on Anglesey by the name of the settlement, Llanddaniel Fab.

20) The story of Arthur's survival reached Spanish culture via Julian del Castillo who reported in 1582 - from a Westcountry sailor? - Arthur's transmigration into a crow, no doubt influencing Cervantes to write of Arthur as a raven in *Don Quixote*. (The chough, crow and raven are all members of the Corvidae. The blood-red colour found in the chough may have influenced the choice of Arthur's reincarnation.)

Is it not therefore of interest that the current President of Venezuela, Nicolas Maduro, claims that his predecessor, Hugo Chavez, to whom he was devoted, visited him in April, 2013 in the form of a bird?

While the Annales Cambriae date (537) is far too late, I feel the curious note in the Historia Brittonum is significant, giving 69 years as the period between the arrival of the Saxons i.e. Hengest, and the consulships of Decius and Valerianus. From 428, this should indicate 496 as the year of the consulships; and we find *from old lists* that Decius Paulinus was believed to be consul in 498. If Paulinus had been misunderstood as & Vlinus, we might be able to explain the phantom Valerianus as an (elastic) expansion of Vlinus. But, asking the question why this date at all, we might feel the compiler of this entry (not the latest one whose name was Nennius) was indicating something now obscured. At any rate, about 20 years after Badon, this is when I place Camlan.[*]

21) There is a second Camelot recorded in one of the early Grail romances. I give the record, in Sebastian Evans' pseudo-Malorian version. His translation of 'The

---

[*] We must remember how texts could be misunderstood especially because of changing scripts, a feature of the post-Roman period.

High History of the Holy Grail' is a marvellous eccentricity, a labour of love too little appreciated. 'Camelot' might conceivably be Carmel Head on Anglesey.

"This Camelot that was the Widow Lady's stood upon the uttermost headland of the wildest isle of Wales by the sea to the West. Nought was there save the hold and the forest and the waters that were around it. The other Camelot, of King Arthur's was situate at the entrance of the kingdom of Logres, and was peopled of folk and was seated at the head of the King's Land, for that he had in his governance all the lands that on that side marched with his own."

22) There is an odd story in the Mirabilia of the Historia Brittonum relating to Arthur's cousin, Illtud. He was in retreat on the coast at Llwynarth in the Gower peninsula of South Wales when two men arrived by boat, bringing the corpse, allegedly of a holy man. They told Illtud they had been instructed by this man to bring him to Illtud; and he was to be buried with him without his name being revealed - to prevent men swearing by him, so they said. So they buried him there. Incidentals about a church and an altar seem to confirm his holiness. But might this be some kind of cover story?

23) The Britons were expelled from Exeter at an uncertain date in Athelstan's reign. Their enclave survived in name until at least the 13th century: *Little Britayne*. It is worth noting what W.G. Hoskins says about the nature of the *latter* period of Saxon conquest: 'Once more we are led back to the possibility that the Saxon occupation and settlement of Devon was a juridical process rather than a military conquest. The English settlers lived under Wessex law, rather than a military conquest. The English settlers lived under Wessex law, paid dues to the kings of Wessex, and as royal tenants enjoyed their direct protection. Their Celtic neighbours, isolated and scattered, lived under Celtic law, paid dues to the kings of Dumnonia, and were under protection for what it was worth. From time to time hostilities broke out, followed usually by a Saxon victory and the extension of Wessex jurisdiction. This is surely what William of Malmesbury means when he says that the Britons and English inhabited Exeter (and presumably also the rest of Devon) *aequo jure*, until Athelstan made an end of their "equality" and caused Wessex law to reign supreme.'

William of Malmesbury's statement about the presence of the British in Exeter provides *the only clear literary evidence* of (probable) continuity of (British) residence in an English city from Roman times through a long period of English occupation.

24) In July of 1998 an archaeologist discovered a broken piece of slate 35 by 20 cm at Tintagel. This appeared to read, in doubtful Latin: Pater Coliavi Ficit Artognou. This may be translated as: 'Arthnou father of Coliaw made this'. In modern dress, it might read: 'Coliaw here commemorates his father Arthnou the builder'. The building is long gone, but Arthnou can be seen as carrying status and belonging to the 6th century. The name Arthnou, its first portion derived from the Brythonic for 'bear', is bound to suggest a link with Arthur's name, he being also originally from Tintagel. It is a fascinating possibility that Arthnou, however remotely, was of the same family as Arthur. But that is all one can really say. I am inclined to another etymology for Arthur's name, distinct also from the commonly accepted Roman 'Artorius'. The Roman word for ploughman was *arator* and passed into Brythonic, whence is derived modern

Welsh *aradwr* or *arddwr*. Is it possible that the Brythonic form was Arddwr? If so, is it coincidence that the modern word for plough is *ylltyd*? And did Illtud's mother name her son with her sister's son in mind?

Tintagel may be linked with St David, patron saint of Wales. Our best evidence is provided by Chrétien de Troyes who, in a long list of Arthurian characters, includes 'Dauit of Tintagel ... who never suffered woe or grief' (*Eric & Enid*). St David is named as Arthur's uncle by Geoffrey, and elsewhere as Arthur's nephew. He belongs to the 6th century, but his background is obscure. There are many Cornish dedications to St David. One collection of the genealogies says his mother's father was Kenyr: this might loosely justify his being called Arthur's nephew, but the claim about his mother is far from the truth. There may be a confusion with some second David who really was a close relative of Arthur's.

25) Sabellicus, born in Vico Varro in Italy, was in his late 60s in 1506 when he died. His *Historia Enneadum*, from which our Romano-British information is derived, was carried down to 1504. Blondus C.1388-1463 was a native of Forli south of Ravenna who wrote *Historiarum Romanarum Decades*.

26) Sigebert's text as given by Ussher runs as follows: 'Britannis subjectionem Romano imperio repromittentibus subsidium misisse Honorium Hispanis Wandalorum bello laborantibus: sed id frustra fuisse.'

27) The Roman rank of consul had existed for many hundreds of years before the 5th century. Why then does the compiler of the Historia Brittonum tell us that consuls 'began' in the time of Magnus Maximus (emperor 383 - 388)? I suggest, because he means the rank began to be used in Britain at that time, having been introduced by Maximus himself.

Vortigern is introduced by Geoffrey in his book VI as *consul* of the Gewissei. This may be connected with the rebellion of a predecessor, Octavius, duke (dux) of the Gewissei, who killed the Roman proconsuls governing Britain. But this is too obscure for comment, except that, we note that Vortigern was Maximus' son-in-law. Another rank is found in this period, first (in historical succession) applied to Maximus: (g)wledic.[*] It probably scarcely survived the 5th century. It has been derived from a Brythonic word for territory. But, given the Roman style of rule that we might reasonably associate with Ambrosius (himself once described as 'son of a consul of the Romanic people'), can't consul and (g)wledic be one and the same? (G)wledic might even be a truncation of some such expression as cons*ul edic*to populi Britanni (or, Romani) i.e. consul by edict of the people of …

At any rate it is surely possible that *(g)wledic* has its origin in *consul*.

---

[*] However, Maximus held no office, according to the historians of the time.

Index of Places and Persons

(as found in the main text and footnotes including Preface)

A

Aberavan 118
Aber Peryddon 120
Adam of Domerham 124, 126
Adrianople 29
Aegidius 36, 37, 38, 54, 94, 99
Aelfthryth (Elfrida) 5
Aelle 86, 87
Aetius, Roman commander 24, 25, 26, 34, 36
Aetius, brother of Merovech 30
Aesc 48
Agned, Mount 57, 59
Agrippinus 41
Ailred of Rievaulx 138
Alaric, Gothic King 29
Alaric II 97
Alfred, King 13, 129
Ambrose, bishop of Milan 23
Ambrosius Aurelianus 22 - 23, 38, 48, 52, 53, 55, 61, 62, 66, 68, 99, 108
Amesbury 118
Amhar 91
Amr (river Gamber) 91
Anblaud 4, 51
Anderida (Pevensey) 87
Aneirin XIV, 42, 131, 132
Angers 96

Anglesey   7, 120
Anguisssance   XI
Anthemius, emperor   61, 63, 64, 96
Arcis   95
Argoed Llwyfain   108
Armorican Tract   27, 28
Arthnou   140
Arthur: Birth and parentage;   4-5
   fostered out;   7
   living beside Bala Lake in Wales with Cei;   8
   to Brittany for education; and marries Leonora?   9-10
   fights with Chlodio?   32-33
   receives his cousin Illtud in the Westcountry?   103-104
   dealings with Aegidius;   37-39
   marries Gwenhwyfar;   51
   returns to make Britain his home?   54-55
   fights successfully with Octa and others;   56-60
   at Déols?   66
   victor in siege of Mount Badon;   67- 69
   peace prevailing, in semi-retirement in the Westcountry;   86-93
   involved in row with Medraut over Gwenhwyfar;   108-113
   fights with Medraut at Camlan and dies;   113-121
   mystery over his burial-place; his coffin found?   121-127
   his Christianity;   134-136
   his humour;   136
   his mistresses;   136-137
   the church's hostility to him   133-134
Arthur map Pedr   132
Arthur son of Aedan   132
Artuir son of Bicoir   132
Artur grandfather of Feradach   132

Arvandus   62
Attila   33, 34, 36
Aurelian, emperor   53
Aurelius Cynon   69
Autun   40
Auvergne   96
Aylesford   21

B

Badbury   69
Badon, Mount   XV, XX, 2, 57, 67-69, 134
Bala Lake   8, 51, 114
Ban   98
Barbury Castle   130
Baschurch   58
Bassas   56, 58
Bassina   97
Bath   52, 130
Bayonne   98
Beaune   98
Beddgeraint   87
Bedd Gwrtheyrn   52
Bede, the Venerable   XV, 131
Bedwyr (Bedivere)   8, 59, 99, 106, 118, 133
Benwick   98
Bican   10, 103
Biedcanford   130
Bilimer   96
Binchester   58, 134
Black Mountains   143
Blaise   138
Bledhericus   138
Blois   97

Bluchbard 42
Blucher 116
Bors of Gaul 98
Bourges 62
Brastias 101
Brest 96
Brewyn (see High Rochester)
Briacat (see Brastias)
Brittenburg 128
Budicius 65
Builth 52

C

Cabeiliauc 51
Cadbury Castle 121
Cadfan, Saint 114
Cadoc, Saint 90, 105, 133
Cador (see Cadwy)
Cadwallaun 7, 102
Cadwy XI, 1, 87, 89, 111, 121
Caer Gai 7
Caer Gybi (Holyhead) 7
Caer Gynyr (see Caer Gai)
Caerleon 58
Cai Hir, Aberavan 118
Camboglanna 113
Cambrai 30
Camel, river 73
Camelford 113
Cameliard (see Cabeiliauc)
Camelot (see Cadbury castle)
Camlan 108 ff, 136
Camlan, near Mallwyd 114

Caradawc Vreichvras   54, 100, 109, 137
Caradoc of Llancarfan   91
Carantoc, Saint   89
Carausius   XIII
Carhampton   89
Carhurles   5
Carnedd Arthur   114
Carveddras   113
Castlesteads (Camboglanna)   113
Catalaunian Plain   34
Cath Paluc   90
Catigern   56
Catraeth (Catterick)   131
Caxton   139
Ceaulin   131
Cei (Kay)   8, 98, 99, 101, 118, 133, 137
Celidon Wood   56, 58
Celli Wig   104, 110, 111, 112, 121
Cerdic of Elmet   XI, 132
Cerdic, K. of West Saxons   129
Châlons-Sur-Marne   34
Chapuys, Eustace   139-140
Chaw Gully   141
Chester   58
Childeric   30, 36, 37, 39, 62, 96
Chirk   52
Chlodio   29, 30, 33
Chlodoveus (see Clovis)
Cian   42-47
Cirencester   130
Cissa   87
City of the Legion   57, 58-59
Claudas   XI, 98
Clovis   97, 98, 128

Conan Meriadoc 31
Constantine, Country of XII
Constantine, Dumnonian regent 1, 88
Constantine, emperor 67
Constantine III 11, 12, 26, 70
Constantius, biographer 69
Constantius, father of Constantine III, 11
Coquet, river 59
Corentin, Saint 9
Coroticus 106
Cornouaille 6
Côtentin XII
Crayford 21, 48
Cribwr 136
Cunedda 136
Custennin (see Constantine, regent)
Cwm Cerwyn 91
Cwm Llan 113, 114
Cwm Tregalan 113
Cynlas 70
Cynric 129

D

Daniel Dremrud 65
Darent, river 21
Dart, river XI
d'Avenches, Marius 39
David, Saint 105
de Glanville, Ranulph 123
de Guise, Jacques 37
Demetia (Dyfed) 128
Déols 63, 96
de Vigneulles, Philippe 37

Devon   XI
Dimilioc   4
Dinas Emrys   53, 113
Dindraithou (Dunster?)   89
Ditchling Cross   86
Dover   119
Drake, Sir Francis   90
Drudwas   137
Dubglas, river   56, 58
Duisburg, Castle of   30
Dumfries   143
Dumnonia   4, 7, 121, 131, 139, 141
Dunwich   110
Dyer, Cutty   90
Dyrham   130

E

Ebbsfleet   16
Ebissa   55
Ecdicius   88
Ector (see Kenyr)
Edgar   5
Edinburgh   XIV
Edwin, king   58, 132
Efflam, Saint   90
Egbert, king   50
Egwine, Saint   125
Eigr   4, 5, 6, 8, 99
Elaine (Helena)   106
Eliman   90
Elizabeth I   112
Elmet   19, 132
Emrys (see Ambrosius)

Erbin 87, 88
Erdudfyl 137
Erging 131
Ermid 111
Essex 22
Essex, Earl of 112
Ethelwerd 13, 86
Ethelwold 5
Eurdeyrn (Outigirn) 131
Euric 61, 62, 63, 66
Eusebius 53
Evesham 125
Ewaine Le Blanchemains 103, 107
Ewein Danwyn 102

F

Faramon (see Pharamond)
Fawkes, Guy 22
Fécamp 123
Felix 26
Fflamddwyn 108, 131
Flodden 58
Flollo 32
Fretiricus 39

G

Galahad 101
Galloway 49
Garwen 137
Gawain (see Gwalchmei)
Genevieve, Saint 95

Geoffrey of Monmouth   XII, XIII, XVI, 4, 31, 39, 112
Geraint, son of Erbin   87, 88, 89
Geraint, 6th century warrior   88
Geraint, 8th century king   89
Germanus   17, 19, 25, 26, 135
Gildas   XV, XVI, 1, 2, 14, 19-20, 23, 42, 67, 69, 70, 91, 92, 102, 108, 129, 130, 133, 134
Giraldus Cambrensis (Gerald of Wales)   122-124, 127, 133, 135
Glamorgan   100
Glastonbury   1, 88,104, 121, 122, 125, 126, 134
Glein, river   56, 57-58
Gloucester   130
Glycerius, emperor   41
Glyndebourne   86
Gorlwys   4, 5, 6, 7
Gormant   4, 6
Gradlon   53
Gregory of Rostrenen, Father   42, 43
Gregory of Tours   30, 39
Guigomar   107
Guinevere (see Gwenhwyfar)
Guinnion, Castle   56, 58, 134, 135
Gundioc   61, 63
Gundleius   105, 133
Guoloppum (see Wallop(s))
Gwalchmai, Anglesey   120
Gwalchmei   49, 55, 100, 107, 119-120, 137
Gwalhafed (see Galahad)
Gwawrddur   XIV
Gwenc'hlan (see Cian)
Gwenhwyfach   110, 111
Gwenhwyfar   51, 101, 110-112, 118, 124, 133-134, 140
Gwerthrynion   52

Gwrgi Garwlwyd   59, 106
Gwron   7
Gwyar   106
Gwydre   91
Gwyl   137
Gwyn the Irascible   111

H

'Hallelujah' Victory   17, 19
Hameldown Ridge   141
Haytor Rocks   141
Hengest   15, 18, 19, 48, 55, 56, 119
'Hengest' placenames   49-50
Henri de Sully   123, 124, 126
Henry of Huntingdon   19
Henry II   122-123
Hereward the Wake   138
Higden, Ranulph   58
High Rochester   59
Honorius, emperor   13, 25
Horsa   15, 21
Horsted   21
Hueil   90, 91, 92, 93, 108, 133
Hydatius   37, 39

I

Iaun Reith   62, 65
Ida   57, 130
Iddawg, son of Mynio   111
Idnerth   102
Igerna (see Eigr)
Igraine (see Eigr)

Illtud, Saint 25, 103, 104, 106
Indeg 137
Indre, river 63
Inscribed Stone, The (Lapis Tituli) 21
Isle of Man (Minau) 92, 93, 108

J

Jordanes 34, 61
Julian, emperor 29
Julius Nepos, emperor 96

K

Kastell Gwalchmei 120
Kenais 103
Kent 17, 21, 49, 68
Kenwyn, Truro 113
Kenyr Keinuarvawc 7, 8
King's Head 141
King's Oven 141
Kit's Coty House 21
Kronos 143
Kynvaur (Cunomorus) 88

L

Lambert of St Omer 55
Lancelot 98
Landévennec 42
Langport 87
Langres 40
Larré 53
Launceston XII

La Villemarqué, Théodore Hersart de   43, 44, 143
Leodegrance (see Ogyrfan)
Leonora   9, 10, 99, 101, 125
Le Pelletier, Dom Louis   42, 43
Leuhan   144
Libius Severus, emperor   39, 40
Liddington Castle   69
Ligessauc Llawhir   90
Lincoln   58
Lindisfarne   131
Linnuis   56, 58
Lionors (see Leonora)
Lissanor (see Leonora)
Llacheu   101
Llamporth   87
Llandudno   137
Llantwit Major   104
Llanwarne   91
Llech Ysgar   101
Lleyn Peninsula   128
Llithfaen   52
Llongborth   87
Llwydeu   91
Llyn Tegid   118
Llŷn, William   111
Llywelyn ap y Moel   118
Loholt   9, 99, 101
Loire, river   62, 63, 64, 96
London   17, 21
Lucan the Butler   XII
Lucius Hiberius   39, 40
Lud   88
Lustleigh   141

M

Madoc 59
Maelgwn Gwynedd 99, 102, 105, 130
Majorian, emperor 36, 38, 39, 40
Malory, Sir Thomas X-XII, XIII, 139
Mangolerian 53
Margawse 106
Marie de France 107
Mark Cross 86
Maximus 11, 15, 27
Mearcraedesburn 36, 108
Medraut (Mordred) 108-116, 117, 119
Melgven 44
Melvas XI, 112, 134
Menez-Bre 44
Merovech 30, 96
Messina, Straits of 107
Milvian Bridge 67
Minehead 120
Moddershall 115
Modena 138
Monnow, river 120
Montgomeryshire 51
Mordred (see Medraut)
Morfran 118
Morgana 103, 106-107, 116

N

Nanmor, Dafydd 118
Nantes 62
Napoleon 116, 144
Natanleod 129

Ninian, Saint 92
Norfolk, Duke of 139

O

Octa 49, 56
Offa's Dyke 52
Ogyrfan 51, 99
Old Sarum 130
Olybrius, emperor 41
Orléans 39
Osfran 114, 118

P

Paris 32, 95
Pascent 52, 102
Pas-de-Paris 30
Patrick, saint 106
Paulinus, (arch) bishop of York 58
Paulus Aurelianus 54, 96
Paulus Diaconus 13
Pellinor XI
Periton 120
Peryddon 120
Petrock, Saint 118
Pevensey (See Anderida)
Pharamond XI, 30
Placidia 26
Poulentus 104, 105
Powys 101, 130
Priscus 30, 37, 40

Q

Queen Camel 122
Quimper 9, 10
Quimperlé 52

R

Rahawd 100
Ralph of Coggeshall 125, 127
Ravenna 12
Rheged 131
Rhos 119, 120
Rica 6
Richard I 123, 126
Ricimer 38, 39, 40, 61, 62, 63, 96
Rienguleid 10, 103
Riocatus 102
Riothamus 62, 63, 64
Riwal 66, 88
Robert of Gloucester 125
Rosemodrass, Boleigh 113
Run Map Urbagen 58
Rushen, Castle 143
Ryons 99

S

Salisbury 52
Saussy 40
Sefin 10
Sevain, Count 9, 10
Severa 15
Sicily 107
Sidonius Apollinaris 64, 65, 96, 102

Sissonne   40
Skokham   120
Skomar   120
Snowdonia   113
Soissons   37, 40, 95, 97
Somerset   XI, 112, 120
Somme, river   30, 95
Stafford   116
St Alban's   XIII
Stamford   19
Stephen, King   XVI
Stone   115
Stow   134
Strathclyde   106, 130, 132
Sussex   22, 86
Syagrius   39, 62, 95, 97

T

Talhaern Tad Awen   42
Taliesin   42, 60, 108, 131
Tancred of Sicily   126
Tegau   137
Tegid   118
Teignweek   XII
Teilo, Saint   130
Terrabil   XI
Thanet   17, 21
Theodoric, Gothic general   128
Theodoric, king   34, 129
Theodosius, emperor   11
Thuringia   37
Tibatto   27-28
Tintagel   4, 140

Toxandria 29
Trearddur Bay 120
Tremodrett 113
Tribruit, river 57, 59, 106
Tristan X
Tryffin 136
Tryvan 118
Twrch Trwyth 47, 91
Tywyn 114

U

Urien of Rheged 60, 131
Uriens of Gore 103, 107
Uther Pendragon 5, 6, 59

V

Valens, emperor 29
Valentinian III, emperor 34
Vale of Avilion 116
Vannes 53, 62, 100
Vertigen 51
Vicus Helena 29
Viroconium 114
Vitalinus 22, 108
Vortigern 15, 16, 18, 22, 23, 31, 51, 131
Vortiporius 8, 128, 132
Vortimer 21, 23, 48, 68

W

Wallingford 51
Wallop (s) 22

Walter, archdeacon of Oxford   XVI, 31
Walwen (see Gwalchmei)
Wansdyke   52
Warren House Inn   141
Waterloo   116
Wedale   134
Wessex   129
West Camel   122
Wigan   58
William the Chaplain   30, 31, 128
William the Conqueror   9
William of Malmesbury   52, 55, 119, 126
Wilmington, the Long Man of   86
Wippedsfleot   24, 48
Wormelow Tump   91
Wrdisten   89
Wroxeter (see Viroconium)
Wulfstan, Saint   8-9

Y

Yarner Wood   141
Yeavering Bell   57
Yorkshire   XI, XIV, 132
Ypwinesfleot   16
Yvain of Cavaliot   99

www.ingramcontent.com/pod-product-compliance
Lightning Source LLC
LaVergne TN
LVHW051544070426
835507LV00021B/2393